Thomas Otway

Twayne's English Authors Series

Bertram H. Davis, Editor

Florida State University

TEAS 335

THOMAS OTWAY
Engraving of Thomas Otway
reproduced by permission of
The Huntington Library
San Marino, California

Thomas Otway

By Kerstin P. Warner

Eastern Kentucky University

Twayne Publishers • Boston

Thomas Otway

Kerstin P. Warner

Copyright © 1982 by G.K. Hall & Company
All Rights Reserved
Published by Twayne Publishers
A Division of G. K. Hall & Company
70 Lincoln Street
Boston, Massachusetts 02111

Book Production by Marne B. Sultz

Book Design by Barbara Anderson

Printed on permanent/durable acid-free
paper and bound in the United States of
America.

**Library of Congress Cataloging in
Publication Data**

Warner, Kerstin P.
Thomas Otway.

(Twayne's English authors series : TEAS
335)
Bibliography: p. 156
Includes index.
    1. Otway, Thomas,
1652–1685—Criticism and
interpretation. I. Title. II. Series.
PR3614.W3   822'.4   82-2952
ISBN 0-8057-6733-9   AACR2

Contents

About the Author

Preface

Chronology

Chapter One
Otway's Life and Legend   1

Chapter Two
Otway's View of the Political Scene (1679–1683)   31

Chapter Three
The First Plays (1675–1678)   58

Chapter Four
Otway's Peak Season (1678–1680)   79

Chapter Five
After the Playhouses Merged (1682–1683)   120

Chapter Six
Conclusion   141

Notes and References   151
Selected Bibliography   156
Index   160

About the Author

Kerstin P. Warner is an associate professor of English at Eastern Kentucky University. Previously she taught English and Humanities at the University of Minnesota, where she received the doctorate and studied under Samuel Holt Monk and Robert Etheredge Moore. She is currently collaborating with Robert A. Sporre on a work dealing with researching and producing Restoration plays.

Preface

It is a curious experience to compare the seven portraits of the Restoration poet and playwright Thomas Otway, wondering which of them could be the most faithful representation of the man who was said to have such "a noble face," "a charming face."[1] The least appealing of the portraits, by John Ryley, may be found in the elderly Mermaid Edition of Otway's plays, edited by Roden Noel. Beneath a tightly curled wig, a square grim face seems to glare through squinting eyes at the beholder. An expression approaching hostility seems to radiate from the set jaw and stubborn lips. Oldys denounces one of Otway's portraits—though not this one—as being too much of a "Quakerish figure," and indeed a stern, sin-sniffing Puritan is what this portrait evokes.[2]

Another portrait shows a fat young man with a puffy face whose eyebrows are faintly raised in an expression of somewhat superior scorn. Because Soest, the painter, died in 1681, Otway must have been in his twenties when this portrait was painted. The excess weight makes him look far older than his years, but then Otway was often lampooned by his contemporaries for his bulk. The eyes may be said to have either a baleful or a contemptuous expression, depending upon the viewer's predisposition. His hair is arranged about his shoulders, with a shorter forelock brushed down over his forehead. This is the portrait which Otway's patron Buckhurst commissioned, and it can be found as the frontispiece to Professor Roswell Gray Ham's biography *Otway and Lee*.

Quite a different aspect is presented in the portrait by Mary Beale. Here Otway is more informally dressed in a shirt, open at the throat, and a comfortable-looking jacket. A pleasant smile turns up his lips, and his right hand casually props his cheek. His hair is brushed away from his face instead of falling in the babyish bangs show in the Soest portrait, and there is a quizzical trace of a frown in the brow. A scroll, lute, dagger-and-crown, tragic mask, and a book are arranged meaningfully beneath the oval frame included in the portrait. Both Soest and Beale carefully depicted a cleft in the poet's chin, which in the latter smiling portrait contributes to the attractive quality of the bemused expression. Mary Beale died in 1697, so the portrait cannot be a product of too great distance from Otway, who died in 1685, though the formal frame embellished with symbolic props suggests that it could well be dedicated to his memory.

The discrepancies of temperament suggested by these portraits appear in Otway's literary reputation and personal legend as well. To some he was the "tender, moving Otway," while others found his work immoral and downright offensive. His competitors lampooned him for his obesity, his poverty, and his penchant for wine. Others engrossed themselves in the passionate love-letters he wrote to the actress Elizabeth Barry, and blamed his entire view of life upon unrequited love. Still others accused him of indulging excessively in self-pity, or pandering to the wealthy in hopes of financial reward. Some, following the attack of Jeremy Collier in 1698, have taken the short view of his plays, condemning them as irreligious and sexually offensive. Others argue that his "mighty line" was incomparable and that his heroic friends and tender lovers were unsurpassed in the history of English drama. He gained a reputation for plumbing the mysterious depths of the female soul and evoking the full range of pity and tenderness, but those who most admired his portrayal of the gentle, sorrowful passions were filled with horror by his explosions of embittered satire and venomous wit.

Because few who have studied his works have been indifferent to the man, a great diversity of opinion exists concerning his true temperament. Otway has been revered and despised, sentimentalized and chastised by critics who, like William Hazlitt, found themselves profoundly moved or vexed—or both—by his work. Dryden wrote enviously of Otway that no one was more capable than he of moving the passions of the soul, and it is true that Otway's psychological insight into passions both tender and gross was remarkable. One of the purposes of this study is to examine his work in the light of psychological theory of his time, the better to appreciate this gift of "moving mightily."

Otway's work also reflects the political struggles of the Restoration, from the terrors of the Popish Plot of 1678 to the tug-of-war between the king and Parliament over the question of excluding James from succession to the throne. In 1678 Otway took up first sword and then pen in defense of the crown. His writings from that date forward respond with the sensitivity of a barometer to the rising and falling pressures of a society which for most of a decade was poised precariously on the verge of civil war. His masterpiece *Venice Preserv'd* is a magnificent study of the moral confusion which is generated by a serious political upheaval. The play transcends partisanship, although Otway was a staunch and outspoken Tory, loyal to the throne and to the true succession, firmly opposed to the ideals and maneuverings of the Puritan Whigs. He well understood the irony of the Chinese curse, "May you live in interesting times." A recurrent theme in his work is the misfortune of writing for an age which is too preoccupied with its political instability to take the time to listen to, much less reward, the special insights of the poet.

Because Otway died young, at thirty-three, and destitute despite the great popularity and success of his plays, the facts of his life and career were quickly transformed into legend, and the revivals of his plays were suffused with gentleness and melancholy pity for the suffering poet. Passages not considered worthy of his lofty genius were excised from the plays. His interest in the psychological sources of all sorts of sexual behavior had been remarkable even for the free-wheeling Restoration, but now a great many passages dealing with psychosexual motivation were deleted. Passages expressing disaffection with government or religion were also deemed inappropriate and were edited. Ultimately these alterations led to still another distortion—the critical interpretation which accuses the now-bowdlerized Otway of mawkish sentimentality and effeminancy of spirit.

It has been especially interesting to study Thomas Otway from the vantage point of the 1980s. The most recent Otway study was Aline Mackenzie Taylor's fascinating stage history *Next to Shakespeare* (1950). Before that there had been a flurry of interest in Restoration drama in the 1920s and early 1930s, which had brought forth two editions of Otway's complete works—those of Montague Summers in 1926 and of J. C. Ghosh in 1932. Ghosh's is the definitive edition, the source of all Otway references in this volume. Between Summers and Ghosh, in 1931, appeared Professor Ham's double biography *Otway and Lee: Biography from a Baroque Age.*

Taylor's review of the revivals of *Venice Preserv'd* prompted her to observe that the political background of the play "is so contrived that it takes on a renewed interest in times of political unrest," while "in times of settled political domesticity, the plot may indeed seem a little 'theatric.' "[3] The last thirty years in the United States have seen the McCarthy hearings, political assassinations, Vietnam war protests, and the Watergate convulsion. In a sense, the churlish allegations of Titus Oates, the desperate general insurrection and assassination plots of the Green-Ribbon men, the rioting at polling-places and terror in the London streets over the Exclusion issue, all have had their recent parallels. In addition, the so-called sexual revolution of the last two decades has made it possible to look at the sexuality in Restoration literature as a manifestation of a view of natural psychology, rather than a sign of either wickedness or frivolous naughtiness.

I wish to express my gratitude to Samuel Holt Monk, who introduced me to *Venice Preserv'd,* and to Robert Etheredge Moore, whose great knowledge of the Restoration theater combined with patience, encouragement, and support to sustain this study. I am grateful to the Huntington Library staff for their perseverance in my behalf. I also wish to thank my husband, John Warner, not only for his personal interest and moral support, but also for the assistance which his own research has provided in taking the drudgery out of evaluating student writing, thereby freeing my time for the completion of this project. Finally, I want to commend Sue Wood for her skilled and patient assistance as a proofreader.

Kerstin P. Warner

Eastern Kentucky University

Chronology

1652 March 3, Thomas Otway born in Woolbeding, Sussex.

1660 Restoration of Charles II to the throne. The two theatrical companies are formed in London.

1668 Otway admitted as one of five commoners to Winchester College.

1669 Otway matriculates at Christ Church, Oxford on May 27.

1670 The role of the King in Mrs. Behn's *The Forc'd Marriage* provokes stage fright in the poet.

1671 Humphrey Otway, his father, dies in February. Otway leaves Oxford.

1675 *Alcibiades* produced at Dorset Garden. King and queen attend a performance of the play on September 22.

1676 *Don Carlos* produced in June. *Titus and Berenice* and *The Cheats of Scapin* appear in December.

1677 *A Session of the Poets* appears, mocking Otway. Otway mistakenly believes the lampoon to have been written by Elkanah Settle.

1678 February 10, Otway is commissioned for the army as an ensign. April, *Friendship in Fashion* is produced. In November, Otway obtains a commission as Lieutenant under Captain William Baggott. Popish Plot.

1679 Exclusion Bill. Shaftesbury promises to serve as "tribune of the people." Otway's company is disbanded, following the Peace of Nymegen. In June, Otway challenges Jack Churchill to a duel after an incident in the playhouse. *Caius Marius* is produced in August or September. Murder of Sir Edmund Berry Godfrey. Pope-burning procession. Monmouth's surprise return from Holland.

1680   *The Orphan* is produced in February or March. *The Poet's Complaint of his Muse* is published in February. *The Soldier's Fortune* is produced in March. On June 1, Otway becomes tutor to Charles Beauclerk, Nell Gwyn's son by the king, for which he is to receive £5,000 per annum. In September, Otway is awarded the M.A. at St. John's College, Cambridge, an honorary degree.

1681   Charles dissolves Parliament at Oxford.

1682   Merger of the two playhouses. *The Tory-Poets* lampoons Otway's love of wine. *Venice Preserv'd* is produced in February.

1683   Rye House Plot discovered. Otway supplies a prologue to Nathaniel Lee's *Constantine the Great*. *The Atheist* is produced, between June and November. Otway begins work on *The History of the Triumvirates*, traslating de Broe.

1684   "Epistle to Mr. Duke" is published.

1685   Charles II dies on February 6. Otway writes the elegy *Windsor Castle* in his memory. Otway dies on Tower Hill on April 14 and is buried on April 16. Robert Gould's "The Playhouse" is published.

1692   Anthony à Wood's *Athenae Oxonienses*.

1697   Otway's love letters to Elizabeth Barry are published in *Familiar Letters*.

1719   *Heroick Friendship,* purporting to be Otway's, appears.

Chapter One

Otway's Life and Legend

Biography and Autobiography

Any discussion of Thomas Otway's life is limited by a shortage of authentic material. We have no journal, only a few love-letters, contracts, statements of debt—and *The Poet's Complaint of His Muse,* an autobiographical poem. Otway's youthful success and popularity as a playwright inspired his enemies to express their envy in witty, scurrilous satires, which can hardly be accepted as historical truth. Eighteenth-century critics, impressed by Otway's ability to write moving and tender scenes, took liberties with the poet's sketchy biography and colored the events of his life with a spurious sentimentality. Nineteenth-century critics inherited these fictions; believing as they did that a man's life and his works were inseparable, they passed the legend along, now embellished with considerable moralizing about the poet's weaknesses and excesses. It is the purpose of this chapter to separate truth from legend, and then place the dubious material in perspective by considering the reasons behind its manufacture.

The Poet's Complaint of His Muse (1680) begins with a description of a happy childhood in the country. The Bard (Otway) says:

> I am a Wretch of honest Race:
> My parents not obscure, nor high in Titles were:
> They left me Heir to no Disgrace.

Humphrey Otway, the poet's father, was the Rector of Woolbeding in Sussex. Born in 1611 the son of Edward Otway, a vicar, he took the M.A. at Christ's College and was ordained a deacon in 1633 and a priest in 1634. In 1638 he became Rector of Woolbeding, where records show that Thomas Otway was born on March 3, 1652. Humphrey Otway died in 1671. Otway's mother, Elizabeth, is known only by her will: she left a silver flagon to the church at Woolbeding, where she died in 1703, thirty-two years after her husband and twenty years after her son. Mrs. Otway left the bulk of her estate to a daughter, Susanna, though the poet never mentions a sister.[1]

Otway enjoyed and excelled in his education, which began at Winchester College, where he was one of five commoners who boarded at the school. In *The Poet's Complaint* he describes himself as a first-rate student, somewhat immodestly:

> When I was call'd to a Dispute,
> My fellow-Pupills oft stood mute:
> Yet never Envy did disjoin
> Their hearts from me, nor Pride distemper mine.

His accomplishments filled his parents' hearts with pride, he says. Winchester was devoted to preparing its students for the universities and therefore eventually for the clergy, and we may fairly assume that Humphrey Otway expected his son to follow in the family profession. At Winchester Otway met Anthony Cary, the fifth Viscount Falkland, who remained his friend through their years together at Oxford and later, when Falkland served as patron for *Caius Marius*.

On May 27, 1669, Otway matriculated at Christ Church, Oxford, where his tutor was Dr. Fell. Probably during a holiday the next year, Otway began his theatrical career by playing the role of the King in Aphra Behn's *The Forc'd Marriage*. It has been noted that the role should be ideal for a novice, requiring as it does the memorization of only 130 lines and very little physically except a dignified presence. But according to the memoirs of John Downes, the prompter for the theater, Otway's acting debut was a disaster.

In this play, Mr. Otway the Poet having an inclination to turn Actor; Mrs. Behn gave him the King in the Play, for a Probation Part, but he being not us'd to the Stage; the full House put him to such a Sweat and Tremendous Agony, being dash't, spoilt him for an Actor.[2]

Otway left Oxford in 1672, two years after his father's death. According to *The Poet's Complaint,* the news "thy good Senander's dead" was a major turning point in his life, driving his "frighted Senses" from their "Feast." Discontent, fears, "and anxious doubts of what I had to do" troubled the poet, increasing with succeeding years until at last he went to London to seek his fortune. Many biographers believe that the "good Senander" must allude to his father, although Montague Summers conjectures that Senander was "some staunch cavalier" who sponsored the promising young man's education and then died in 1672, forcing Otway's withdrawal from the university.[3] Whoever Senander was, the psychological crisis caused by his death profoundly changed Otway's life. The clever Oxford student who was preparing traditionally for the clergy turned about and left the university to gamble on his future in London "where Fortune's generall Game is play'd."

Though Otway himself does not mention it, two of his contemporary biographers, Anthony à Wood and Charles Gildon, agree that he worked for a time as an actor. *The Poet's Complaint* describes an initiation period of feeding "on every sort of Vanity," mingling with fools and mimicking their follies, and being "by raw Judgment easily miss-led." This passage and others have led the moralizing biographers to assume that Otway was a libertine, drinking, wenching, and roistering like Lord Rochester and his wild companions. But the poem suggests that this interlude was useful in leading him to his Muse.

Otway conceives of his Muse as a glamorous but deceitful mistress, and he compares the discovery of his poetic ability to the euphoria of a first love affair.

I must confess, I had a Tittilation to Poetry, but never durst venture on my Muse, till I got her into a Corner in the Country, and then like a bashful young lover, when I had her in private, I had Courage to fumble, but never thought she would have produc'd anything, till at last, I know not how, e're I was aware I found myself the Father of a Dramatique birth, which I call'd *Alcibiades*.[4]

In *The Poet's Complaint*, his Muse appears to him all bedecked with jewels, gold, and pearls, wearing a crown of laurel (the coveted prize of poetry), beckoning to him and promising him riches—"Riches which never Poet had before." This is the first sign of her falsity, for we know the bitter truths about Otway's meager earnings as a playwright. But the affair, at least at first, was exhilarating: Otway describes making love to her every time they met, enjoying limitless potency, being "blest with Off-springs of the choicest kinds."

Alcibiades and *Don Carlos* were presumably these offspring. We know that *Alcibiades* was produced at Dorset Garden in September 1675, and that the king and queen attended the play on September 22. The play was dedicated to Lord Buckhurst, then the Earl of Middlesex, who apparently responded to the favor with a generous gift of cash, as well as arranging for Soest to paint Otway's portrait.[5] The play itself was standard heroic drama in rhymed verse, and though the title figure was somewhat more obtuse than was usual even for a Restoration hero, for a maiden effort it received satisfactory approval.

Don Carlos, however, was a great success. Otway's Muse was still favoring him, apparently, for this play was produced the very next spring in late May or early June 1676, at Dorset Garden. According to John Downes, the prompter, *Don Carlos* "got more money than any preceding Modern Tragedy."[6] Dedicated to the king's brother, the Duke of York, it ran for ten successive days and was frequently revived for the next fifty years. The plot was drawn from a fictionalized historical account of Don Carlos written by the French historian Saint-Real, and the action focuses upon an intolerable triangle involving an elderly king, his young bride, and his young son Don Carlos. The real significance of the triumph is that Otway was now taken seriously as a writer and envious wits paid attention enough to attack and lampoon him in the cruel but customary style of the Restoration literary circles. Even the established poet John Dryden took note of the play by disdainfully claiming that there was not a single line of "which he would care to acknowledge himself the author."[7] The anonymous satire, attributed to Rochester, *The Tryal of the Poets for the Bays,* is merciless:

> Tom O—— came next, Tom S——'s dear Zany,
> And swears for Heroicks he writes best of any;
> Don C—— his Pockets so amply had fill'd,
> That his Mange was quite cur'd and his Lice were
>   all kill'd.
> But Apollo had seen his Face on the Stage,
> And prudently did not think fit to engage
> The Scum of a Play-House for the Prop of an Age.[8]

Otway was insulted by the poem, which he believed to have been written by Elkanah Settle, and felt morally obliged to seek revenge.

Gossip, malicious and benign, seemed to generate spontaneously around the Restoration theater and its celebrities, for plays were immensely fashionable in court circles because the king was himself a "fan." Indeed, the lore and gossip concerning actors, actresses, playwrights and patrons rivals in abundance today's fascination with the world of filmmaking. Some of today's movie stars seem resigned to vicious rumors as part of the business of fame, a nuisance, perhaps, but useful publicity. Nell Gwyn and Elizabeth Barry managed to cope rather calmly with such matters, but not the playwrights and certainly not Otway. *Don Carlos* brought down upon Otway's head a barrage of vicious attack, which not only took him by surprise but embittered him for the rest of his days.

During the summer of 1676, Otway was busy putting together a double bill which would be presented in the Duke's Theater in December. These two short plays were adaptations from the French, *Titus and Berenice* being drawn from Racine's *Berenice,* and *The Cheats of Scapin,* from Molière's *Les Fourberies de Scapin.* Otway was racing against time for he knew that John Crowne was working on a version of *Berenice,* to be called *The Destruction of Jerusalem,* and Ravenscroft was combining *Le Mariage Forcé* and *Les Fourberies de Scapin* for the other playhouse. Otway and the Duke's Theater won the race and were not forgiven for their arrogance. Crowne's play appeared in January 1677 and was a great success, but Otway's *Cheats,* featuring the delightful comic actor Tony Leigh, was not surpassed. Although he achieved notoriety for the feat and was treated to more lampooning for his insolence, these plays were not original enough to be considered anything more than potboilers, to put a little money in his pocket.

It was quite likely about this time that he suffered the crisis which he described thoroughly in *The Poet's Complaint*:

> All of a sudden I was alter'd grown,
> I round me lookt, and found my self alone:
> My faithless Muse, my faithless Muse was gone.

Her sudden desertion caused him agony. He tried to write, but produced lines monstrous in their birth, and his misery was unrelenting:

> I found m'ungratefull Muse, for whose false sake
> I did myself undo,
> Had robb'd me of my dearest Store,
> My precious Time, my Friends, and Reputation too;
> And left me helpless, friendless, very proud,
>   and poor.

Most biographers, oddly enough, ignore this passage though it describes a crucial disillusionment. The complaining poet confers with Reason (a male figure, interestingly), who claims to be glad to be restored to the poet's mind. When asked why this disaster should have befallen him, Reason explains that the Muse never stays with writers whom Fortune deserts, "for Fortune is a Bawd / To all the Nine that on Parnassus dwell." Reason then lifts "the veil of Dotage" from the poet's eyes and shows him his Muse as she truly is, a "rampant, tawdry Quean," followed by a vile train of sycophants.

In enumerating the Muse's nasty lovers, all poets unworthy of fame, Otway has an opportunity to pay back his satirists. First in line is the author of the "Sodom farce," a play too pornographic even for Restoration tastes, which had apparently been performed before the king and a mixed audience by nude actors. Nobody knows who wrote *Sodom,* though it has been unconvincingly attributed to Rochester, probably because of his libertine reputation. Since Otway satirizes Rochester separately here, we may assume that he was not the author in question, "raven'd by old diseases." Next in line is Elkanah Settle, "that blundring Sot / Who a late Sessions of the Poets wrote." He is compared to an owl who loves the night, who "repeats dull plays . . . for old shoes and scraps." Otway believed Settle to be responsible for the allusion to his mange and his lice. Next comes Rochester, "Lord Lampoon and Monsieur Song," who offers court favors to the tawdry Muse: though unbeknownst to Otway, he quite possibly was the one who called him "the Scum of the Playhouse." Last there is the City-Poet, one Thomas Jordan, whose duty it was to compose pageants and complimentary poems for even the dullest of London occasions, praising whoever happened to be lord mayor at the time. As the poet watches Reason's masque, the Muse proffers her favors to her retinue, and "they took her all by turns aside."

At this point in his life, for the first time, Otway feels that Fortune has turned on him. Publicly mocked by wags and wits, he sees bad plays achieving greater popularity than good ones, and realizes that he has lost time, friends, reputation—and money. This allegory of love, betrayal, and disillusionment, though it applies on one level to his dramatic career, is consciously expressed in the terms of a sexual relationship because he had fallen in love with Elizabeth Barry when she played the confidante in his *Alcibiades*. Though he courted her with impassioned letters, she was interested in him only as a friend (and creator of leading roles). When she played Berenice's confidante in December 1676 she had already become Lord Rochester's mistress and was soon to be pregnant with his daughter. Despite her explanation that she had bound her affections with another man, Otway felt betrayed, injured, and outraged by her lack of interest in him. The bitterness expressed toward the Muse in *The Poet's Complaint* is precisely comparable to the emotion we shall find when we look later at the love-letters and the ensuing legend.

"My faithless Muse, my Faithless Muse was gone." The case of writer's block probably overtook Otway shortly after the production of his double bill, for between December 1676 and April 1678 he brought forth no new plays. The comedy *Friendship in Fashion* which then appeared is different from anything he had written before. It is a witty, cruel satire of marriage and sexual mores among people of fashion, and it earned Otway a new reputation for obscenity, because at least three sexual associations take place during the course of the play and half a dozen more are alluded to. Though assuredly not so explicit as *Sodom* in terms of what is seen on stage, *Friendship in Fashion* leaves no doubt in the audience's mind concerning what is going on in the shadows of the rose garden. The plot is an elaborate bawdy joke and the lines are as polished and poised as dueling swords. Otway wrote the part of the sexually opportunistic wife specifically for Mrs. Barry, but he never saw her performance because he suddenly joined the army.

Financial Troubles

Records show that he obtained a commission on February 10, 1678, as an ensign in a regiment which was sent to Flanders. He was appointed lieutenant to one Captain William Baggott on the first of November of that year, but these troops were almost immediately disbanded by the House of Commons, which was ever fearful that

Charles might be surreptitiously trying to increase his militia. For this brief service to his country, Otway received a note of debenture for £27.17.6 which proved to be unnegotiable for over a year.[9] One of his characters in *The Soldier's Fortune* sums up the poet's own experiences following the peace of Nymegen.

Fortune made me a soldier, a Rogue in Red, the grievance of the Nation, Fortune made the peace just when we were upon the brink of a War; then Fortune disbanded us, and lost us two Months pay; Fortune gave us Debentures instead of ready Money, and by very good Fortune, I sold mine, and lost heartily by it, in hopes that the ill natur'd dog that bought it will never get a shilling for't.

Hopes of relieving his poverty were dashed, as was his faith in the Parliament which had treated him so shabbily, and he was forced to find and pay his own way back to London. So in Flanders he had begun the draft of a play, while he still "had nought but Drums and Trumpets in his Head." This was *Caius Marius,* a curious mixture of Shakespeare's *Romeo and Juliet* and Plutarch's tale of revolution. *Caius Marius* ranks third in popularity of Otway's plays, after *Venice Preserv'd* and *The Orphan,* for it played successfully nearly every season for the next fifty years after its first production in late autumn 1679.

Politics lay behind Otway's unpleasant army experience, and politics was dividing the poets, as it divided the nation in general, into hostile factions. The civil disorder portrayed in *Caius Marius* reflected the unsettled times, and certainly this political relevance contributed to the success of the play. Just as *The Poet's Complaint* shifts in the middle from autobiography to an allegorical satire against the Protestant Whigs, we find a new contentiousness in Otway at this point in his career.

The Otway-Settle conflict, according to one obviously biased account, very nearly came to blows:

And Mr. O. a man of the Sword, as well as the Pen, finding himself most coursly dealt withal, immediately call'd him to an account, and required the satisfaction of a Gentleman from him: This I must confess was something unreasonable, and did by no means agree with our Scriblers Constitution, who had much rather Rail than Fight.[10]

This tale further alleges that Settle pleaded for his life, confessed to writing the poem, and called himself "the Son of a W——— for doing it." Settle's response in 1683, "In Reply to the Dulnes and Malice of Two Pretended Answers to that Pamphlet," denies all—the authorship as well as being a son of a W——. This tempest is alluded to in Shadwell's *Tory Poets* of 1628: "S——'s a Coward, 'cause fool Ot—y fought him."[11]

A report of June 23, 1679, tells how "Captain" Otway drew his sword in the Duke's Playhouse in challenge of Jack Churchill, the future Duke of Marlborough:

Churchill, for beating an orange wench in the Duke's playhouse, was challenged by Capt. Otway (the poet), and were both wounded, but Churchill most.[12]

Otway's most productive season followed, for in the first three months of the next year, he brought forth *The Orphan, The Poet's Complaint,* and *The Soldier's Fortune.* It is more than a little ironic that a writer of at least three very successful plays should be wanting for funds, particularly at this prolific time in his career. But political difficulties combined with the transitional economic state of the theaters to conspire against any hopes a dramatist might have of becoming rich. *Don Carlos* had been a great financial success, but from the time of the production of *Caius Marius,* Otway regularly complains of money problems. The *Epilogue* to *Caius Marius* is typical:

> Our Poet says, one day to a Play ye come,
> Which serves ye half a year for Wit at home.
> But which amongst you is there to be found,
> Will take his third day's Pawn for Fifty pound?

Proceeds from the third night's performance of a play went to the author. When we recall that Otway wrote only nine plays in eight years, it is not difficult to see that the offer to trade his third night's income for an "advance" of £50 was plainly unattractive and a desperate concession to the need to survive. The *Epilogue* continues, alluding to the worthless debenture paper from the army:

> Or, now he is Cashier'd will fairly venture
> To give him ready Money for's Debenture?
> Therefore when he receiv'd that Fatall Doom,
> This play came forth, in hopes his Friends would come
> To help a poor Disbanded Souldier home.

Gildon's allusion to the financial insecurity of Restoration dramatists, although primarily intended to illustrate what he considers to be the practical improvements in such matters in his own time (1721), may shed some light on Otway's problems, though we have no way of ascertaining the accuracy of the figures stated here:

We have had extraordinary Encouragement for Dramatick Poetry, and that much greater than ever had been known before in this nation, which however has not been able to produce any valuable performance in that way; and several Authors have made from three and four hundred Pounds to fifteen hundred for one Tragedy or Comedy; which however never reached a second Season. Whereas Otway, Lee, and Dryden could never attain more for one piece than one hundred Pounds.

Gildon's analysis continues with an allusion to the plays of Nathaniel Lee, who died in the street during a period of release from Bedlam.

I believe by a fair Computation, that *Mithridates, Theodosius, Alexander the Great,* and *Hannibal,* have gain'd the several actors that have succeeded each other not less than fifty thousand pounds, and yet the author scarce got one hundred pounds a piece for his labour, and dy'd at last in the very street; whereas if our English great men, who had power to have done it; had fix'd and order'd that the Poet should have receiv'd a reasonable share of the profits of his plays as long as they were acted in his time, as it is in France, he had had a comfortable maintenance from his labors, and escap'd that miserable fate that befel him. Thus, Otway had but a hundred pounds apiece for his *Orphan* and *Venice Preserv'd,* tho' the players, reckoning down to this time, have not got less than twenty thousand pounds by them.[13]

We know that Otway was preoccupied with finding patronage even before he sailed for Flanders, when in the dedication of *Friendship in Fashion* he apologizes for being "remiss . . . in my respects to your Lordship, in that I have not waited on you so frequently as the duty I owe your Lordship and my own Inclinations required; But the Circumstances of my Condition, whose daily business must be daily Bread, have not, nor will allow me that happiness." Later, the prologue to *Caius Marius* expresses envy of Shakespeare's security:

> Our Shakespeare wrote too in an Age as blest,
> The happiest Poet of his time and best.

> A gracious Prince's Favour chear'd his Muse,
> A constant Favour he ne'er fear'd to lose.

Otway was decidedly not secure in his patronage. Apart from his school friend Falkland, he seems to have had no constant support, and Falkland it is said was "nearly as indigent as the poet himself."[14] His early patron, Rochester, backed him for only a short time. Buckhurst, who was perhaps most generous toward him, withdrew his support when *Friendship in Fashion* was rumored to contain caricatures of members of the court. Two other patrons, Plymouth and Ossory, died before 1680. The king's mistresses were generous but unreliable. The Duchess of Portsmouth reportedly gave Otway twenty guineas for the compliment of *Venice Preserv'd,* and Nell Gwyn sent her son to be tutored by Otway when he was particularly impecunious.

The patronage system in general was breaking down. It was unsatisfactory to the authors who resented heaping flowery compliments upon noblemen who in their turn often resented the obligation to pay for the gratuitous praise. Upon this latter situation, Ravenscroft comments:

No person of Quality, how remote soever, can escape the Impertinences of Poets; for though they be Hundreds of miles off, they shall be pursu'd and persecuted with Dedicatories o're and o're, even by the same Authors. . . . But this is excusable in them that Write for Bread and live by Dedications, and Third-Days. If once in a Year they meet not with a good Audience, or a bountiful Maecenas, we are to expect no play from them the next. . . .[15]

At one point Otway broke with tradition and wrote a remarkably plainspoken dedication to Richard Bentley, his printer:

For, Mr. Bentley, you pay honestly for the Copy; and an Epistle to you is a sort of an Acquittance, and may be probably welcome; when to a Person of higher Rank and Order, it looks like an Obligation for Praises, which he knows he does not deserve, and therefore is very unwilling to part with ready money for.[16]

Toward the end of his short life Otway was apparently threatened by debtors' prison. "Otway can hardly Gutts from Gaol preserve, / For tho' he's very fat, he's like to Starve."[17] Yet another allusion to this phenomenon is found in "A Supplement to the Late Heroick Poem":

> Lift up your Heads ye Tories of the Age,
> Let Otway tumble Shadwell from the Stage,
> Otway who long (leane loyalty preserving)
> Has shown a wonder and grown fat with starving.[18]

In 1682, for economic reasons, the two London playhouses merged,
creating another crisis for dramatists by severely reducing the chances
for bringing forth new plays. Many dramatic writers, including Otway,
were forced to "diversify" by trying their hands at translation. The
Satyr on the Modern Translators summarizes their difficulties:

> Those who with Nine Months Toil had spoil'd a Play
> In hopes of eating at a full Third Day,
> Justly despairing longer to sustain
> A craving Stomach from an empty Brain,
> Have left Stage-practice, chang'd their old Vocations,
> Attoning for bad Plays, with worse Translations.[19]

A chronological reading of Otway's prologues and epilogues, with an
eye to tracing the development of his attitudes toward his profession,
proves to be revealing. In 1675, at the beginning of *Alcibiades,* the
novice playwright defers to the audience, meekly expressing the wish
that "Since Non-sence is so generally allow'd, / He hopes that his own
may pass amongst the Crowd." In his second play he asks the audience
for criticism:

> Prune his superfluous Branches, never spare;
> Yet do it kindly, be not too severe,
> He may bear better fruit another year.

Such modesty is not to last, however. After 1678, the critical year of his
misadventure in Flanders, two favorite themes emerge. One takes the
form of a series of attacks upon the idiotic presumption of the coxcombs
in the pit, who think they know what a good play should be, and the
other is the complaint, not unrelated, that being a poet in this age is a
miserable occupation.

> Who'd be a Poet? Parents all beware,
> Cherish and Educate your Sons with care:
> Breed 'em to wholsome Law, or give 'em Trades,
> Let 'em not follow the Muses, they are Jades.

He begins to complain about money in the epilogue to *Caius Marius,* as we have noted, and in the prologue to *The Orphan* he takes up his favorite theme of libel and sedition. But the culmination of his bitter anger against the abuses of his profession appears in the prologue he wrote for Nathaniel Lee's *Constantine the Great.* The story behind the production of this play is interesting: *Constantine* is conjectured to have been a revision of something Lee had begun writing years before, when he was employing his high-flown heroic style. Because the play lacks a dedication, the prologue was contributed by Otway and the epilogue by Dryden, and shortly after its publication Lee was confined once again in Bedlam. Professor Ham argues that Lee's friends in the theater rallied to help him by putting the play together for him.[20] Whether this is so or not, it would not be untoward to assume that Otway has Lee's anguish as well as his own in mind when he begins the prologue with one of his invariably grim meditations upon Providence.

> What think ye meant wise Providence, when first
> Poets were made? I'd tell you, if I durst,
> That 'twas in Contradiction to Heaven's Word. . . .

He continues, citing the fate of starvation as evidence that a poet is "unnatural," a wretched mutation.

> For, were it worth the Pains of six long Days,
> To mould Retailers of dull Third-Day-Plays,
> That starve out threescore Years in hopes of Bays?
> 'Tis plain they ne're were of the first Creation,
> But came by meer Equiv'cal Generation.
> Nature their Species sure must needs disown.

With thoroughgoing contempt, Otway once again attacks the aristocratic amateurs who are invading the writing profession.

> The Poet and the Whore alike complains,
> Of trading Quality, that spoils their Gains;
> The Lords will write, and Ladies will have Swains.

He concludes with a startlingly scatological warning to all parents whose children think they want to be poets, clearly alluding to himself:

> Therefore, all you who have Male Issue born,
> Under the starving Sign of Capricorn:
> Prevent the Malice of their Stars in time,
> And warn them early from the Sin of Rhime:
> Tell 'em how Spencer starv'd, how Cowley mourn'd,
> How Butler's Faith and Service was return'd;
> And if such Warning they refuse to take,
> This last Experiment, O Parents, make!
> With Hands behind them see the Offender ty'd,
> The Parish Whip, and Beadle by his side.
> Then lead him to some Stall that does expose
> The Authors he loves most, there rub his nose;
> Till like a Spaniel lash'd, to know Command,
> He by the due Correction understand,
> To keep his Brains clean, and not foul the Land.

Such is the frame of mind of "kind-hearted Otway" not long before his death.

We can understand, therefore, why Otway on June 1, 1680, took the job of tutor to Charles Beauclerk, the young son of Nell Gwyn and the king. A record shows that Otway was under contract for payment of £5,000 per annum for preparing the boy for college. Recalling the small sums mentioned earlier, it appears that at least for this year, Otway had a chance of living in some comfort. Jealousy prompted the author of *An Essay of Scandal* to jeer at this arrangement:

> Then for that Cubb her Son and Heire
> Lett him remaine in Otway's care
> To make him (if that's possible to be)
> A viler Poet, and more dull than he.[21]

Otway's signature appears at this time on a legal document transferring Nell Gwyn's power of attorney to one James Fraizer of Westminster.[22]

It is also on record that Otway received the M.A. degree from St. John's College, Cambridge, in 1680.[23] Since there are no records of his ever having been admitted there, it seems reasonable to guess that this was an honorary degree.[24] It is also likely that Otway had retired to Cambridge with his pupil. His good friend Richard Duke was teaching at Cambridge, and Otway later wrote him a pleasant poem, "Epistle to R.D. from T.O.," celebrating a long, relaxing visit.

During the last half of 1681 he began work on *Venice Preserv'd,* his most important tragedy based on Saint-Real's *La Conjuration des Espagnols contre la Republique de Venise.* This play, which was performed first early in 1862, was dedicated to the Duchess of Portsmouth, the king's mistress and Nell Gwyn's rival. The dedication apparently brought an abrupt end to the actress's support of the playwright. It is unfortunate that, though *Venice Preserv'd* was a brilliant success, once again the financial reward was minimal.

From this point on, biographical facts are scarce. Otway's last comedy, *The Atheist,* was produced in 1683. It is an oddly confused play with an unfinished quality about it, and like his other comedies, it was considered highly controversial. Also in 1683 he wrote the scatalogical prologue to Lee's *Constantine,* and in 1684 published the "Epistle to Mr. Duke."

Reports of Otway's condition at this time must be gathered obliquely from local gossip. He is noted as having trouble with his creditors: "Otway can hardly Gutts from Gaol preserve."[25] Among others, he owed money to Jacob Tonson the publisher, to Betterton the actor, and a rather large sum to one Captain Symonds, a vintner.[26] Shadwell's portrait of Otway in *The Tory Poets* of 1682 accuses him of being able to write only when drunk: "Wine does now the Poets breast inspire, / . . . Wine, that makes Ot—y write and Fools admire."[27]

Between 1683 and 1685, Otway undertook to write a translation of a work of French history, *A History of the Triumvirates* by Sieur de Broe.[28] This work, along with *Windsor Castle,* an elegy on the recent death of King Charles, appeared posthumously. Six of his tortured love-letters to Elizabeth Barry, assigned by Professor Ham to 1681 and 1682, were also published after his death.

Love Letters

The love letters present an account of an extremely painful passion. They are worth examining closely if only because Otway's great female characters have such great power over his heroes and, possibly as a result, are the objects of a fascinating mixture of love and hatred. In his letters to Barry the same ambivalence surfaces.

Mrs. Barry's career was intimately linked with Otway, if her affections were not. She had played Draxilla in *Alcibiades,* two roles in the double bill, Mrs. Goodvile in *Friendship in Fashion,* and Lavinia (Juliet) in *Caius Marius.* She was the orphan Monimia, and played the role until she was an old woman, long after Otway was dead. She played Lady Dunce in *The Soldier's Fortune,* Belvidera in *Venice Preserv'd,* and Porcia in *The Atheist.* She was the actress whom he had very much in mind when he wrote his great plays, and so in a sense she seemed to him partly his creation. He fell in love with her—or with his creation—and wrote accusing her of having enslaved him:

Your Commands have always been sacred to me; your Smiles have always Transported me, and your Frowns aw'd me. In short, you will quickly become to me the greatest Blessing, or the greatest Curse, that ever Man was doom'd to.

Mrs. Barry replied to this letter explaining that her affection was already committed to another man and offering her friendship in lieu of love. Exasperated by this rejection, Otway vowed that despite the existence of a rival he was determined to hope.

I have consulted too my very self, and find how careless Nature was in framing me; seasoned me hastily with all the most violent Inclinations and Desires, but omitted the Ornaments that should make those Qualities become me: I have consulted too my Lot of Fortune, and find how foolishly I wish possession of what is so pretious, all the World's too cheap for it, yet still I love, still I dote on, and cheat my self, content because the Folly pleases me.

Then, suddenly angered at the offer of friendship, "gross, thick, homespun Friendship," he sarcastically directs her to go trade herself for money: "give it the Man who would fill your lap with Gold." He accuses her of barring only him from her favors—and then he begs for charity.

In a later letter Otway charges that Mrs. Barry has made him appear ridiculous. When calling on her one morning, he was told that she was not in, and so he instantly concluded that she must be entertaining another man. Convinced that she plotted ways to torture him, he complains:

Your whole Bus'ness is to pick ill-natur'd Conjectures out of my harmless freedom of Conversation, to vex and gall me with, as often as you are pleased to DIVERT your self at the expense of my Quiet. Oh thou Tormentor! Could I think it were Jealousie, how should I humble myself to be justify'd, but I cannot bear the thought of being made a Property either of another Man's good Fortune, or the Vanity of a Woman that designs nothing but to plague me.

This fifth letter closes with a threat: "There may be means found sometime or other, to let you know your mistaking."

Otway seems to be living Castalio's misery in *The Orphan*. At first Castalio finds in Monimia all the perfection of nature:

> Where am I! surely Paradise is round me!
> Sweets planted by the hand of Heaven grow here,
> And every sence is full of thy Perfection.

He marries her in a secret ceremony, but his envious twin brother, Polydore, contrives to impersonate him in the bridal chamber. Through a combination of Polydore's lustfulness and Monimia's improbable ignorance (all twins are identical in the dark), Castalio is turned away from his bride's room to ponder the incredible wickedness of women. His eloquent diatribe perfectly matches Otway's own anguish over being turned away from Mrs. Barry's door:

> Destructive, damnable deceitful Woman.
> Woman to Man first as a Blessing giv'n,
> When Innocence and Love were in their Prime,
> Happy a while in Paradise they lay,
> But quickly Woman long'd to go astray,
> Some foolish new Adventure must needs prove,
> And the first Devil she saw she chang'd
>   her Love,
> To his Temptations lewdly she inclin'd
> Her Soul, and for an Apple damn'd Mankind.

The contempt, though born of injury, implicit in these letters could not be expected to provoke fond capitulation on the part of the woman to whom they are addressed. Being accused of trading favors for cash, or of being everybody's mistress but his, even in the worldly Restoration is not likely to stimulate a warm, affectionate response.

Most of Otway's biographers take their cue from these letters and from Robert Gould's "The Playhouse," composed in the year of the poet's death, and assert that Elizabeth Barry is wholly responsible for his suffering, unworthy as she is of his admiration. Gould calls Barry "a ten times cast off Drab, in Venus' Wars / Who counts her Sins, may as well count the Stars," and adds that "She'l prostitute with any, / Rather than waive the getting of a penny."[29] From this perspective, one might be led to assume that her rejection of Otway's frenzied petitions was merely a combination of mercenary interest and a hard heart. Montague Summers in 1926 enthusiastically takes sides: "Mrs. Barry, I doubt not, was hard as adamant, and possibly sexless. I imagine she was the perfect whore."[30] Seven years after his poem had extensively undertaken to count her sins, Robert Gould was taken aback when Mrs. Barry refused to perform in a tragedy he had written, and was even more surprised that Betterton, backing her up, refused to produce it. "I am not so good a Christian as to forgive," was Mrs. Barry's simple explanation.

One might expect that she had shown similar self-respect in her rejection of Otway's ambivalent protestations of love, especially when we recall that he accused her of picking "ill-natur'd Conjectures" out of his "harmless Conversation." Otway seems to be feeling many of the emotions he gives his heroes—a sense of enslavement, a mixture of helpless adoration and violent resentment of that helplessness, to the extent of paradoxically wishing vicious punishment upon his mistress. We must keep in mind that he declares that he finds pleasure in this painful, masochistic "folly of love."

Furthermore, nobody could know Otway's highest idea of love better than Elizabeth Barry who had, after all, been its object in most of his plays. It is more than likely that she knew precisely how to play her role in dealing with his passion for her. Monimia and Belvidera would not succumb to the importunings of a man they did not love: they have to be raped. They are accustomed to earth-shattering protestations of love. It is of course conjecture, but it seems plausible that the story behind the love letters involves an emotional and psychological understanding which existed between Otway and Barry, which necessitated unrequited feeling.

With this in mind, let us imagine what lay behind the sixth and final letter:

You were pleased to send me word you would meet me in the Mall this Evening, and give me further satisfaction in the Matter you were so unkind to charge me with; I was there, but found you not, and therefore beg of you, as you would wish your self to be eased of the highest Torment it were possible for your Nature to be sensible of, to let me see you some time to Morrow, and send me word by this Bearer, where, and at what hour you will be so just as either to acquit or condemn me: that I may hereafter, for your sake, either bless all your bewitching Sex; or as often as I henceforth think of you, curse Womankind for ever.

Otway's ambivalence is never clearer. On his side, he claims to be unjustly charged with an offense: when she summons him to hear his defense, he comes but finds her not there. He demands another appointment and threatens to decide his future opinion of her entire sex upon the basis of her decision. He makes Mrs. Barry an arbitrary goddess of justice who holds his fate in her whimsical hands. There is even scorn in his apparently innocent pleading for her use of the Golden Rule: "as you would wish your self to be eased of the highest Torment it were possible for your Nature to be sensible of" simultaneously begs for fairness, hints at a limited sensibility on her part, and indulges in a fantasy of seeing her tortured. Such complexity of emotion and language assists us in understanding Jaffeir's furious, impassioned outburst in *Venice Preserv'd*: "Oh thou wert born either to save or damn me."

The Legends Begin: Lost Masterpieces

Charles II died on February 6, 1685, and Otway died on April 14 of that year. *Windsor Castle,* which mourns the late king and expresses hope for the reign of his brother James, must therefore have been written in the last two months of the poet's life. Charles's last seizure and death caused a good deal of national upheaval, of course, but Otway died in obscurity. There are so many different reports of the circumstances of his death that one may only conclude that the true story will never be known. This much is certain: his Strumpet Fortune had abandoned him. As Montague Summers observed, "The manner of his death . . . is hardly uncertain, since it seems only too assured that he expired in extreme indigence, misery, and neglect."[31]

Otway's death at the age of thirty-three was a surprise and a shock to those who had known him as well as those who merely admired his plays. He had dropped from sight before, we know, to retreat to Cambridge to write, and so it is possible that no one had missed him since *The Atheist* was produced in 1683. News of his death at so young an age, combined with the recollection of the splendid plays he had written in his twenties, seems to have positively inspired people to create stories explaining the mystery of these last two years. To a literary historian these legends are fascinating in their own right for a multitude of reasons. But a biographer can only cite the parish register at the church of St. Clement Danes, which simply states, "1685. Thomas Otway, a man, buried 16 April."

There was a persistent rumor that he was working on his greatest tragedy ever, *Heroick Friendship,* at the time of his death. This was given substance by an advertisement which appeared a year and a half later, on November 29, 1686, in the *Observator*:

Whereas Mr. Thomas Otway some time before his death made four Acts of a Play, whoever can give notice in whose hands the copy lies, either to Mr. Thomas Betterton, or to Mr. William Smith at the Theatre Royal shall be well rewarded for his pains.[32]

By then, of course, it was much too late to have any real hope of finding this manuscript, if indeed it ever existed. One must assume that the legend-makers were responsible for the rumor, which provoked the soft-hearted Oliver Goldsmith to give it credence and to mourn, "What an invaluable treasure was there irretrievably lost by the ignorance and the neglect of the age he lived in!"[33]

In 1719, or thirty-four years after Otway's death, a play purporting to be *Heroick Friendship* appeared. In structure it resembles *Alcibiades,* but in the awkwardness of its verse it is unsurpassed. For example, when the lady Aurosia expresses her fears that her beloved Guiderius will die, she utters the following nonsense:

> . . . Yes thou goest to die;
> And did not stronger Circumstance convince me,
> Yet there is something in thy Words and Actions,
> As tells me I shall never see thee more.[34]

Apart from the poetry, another damning bit of internal evidence is the fact that Fortune is alluded to as a male: "till Fortune's weary grown, / Repents his Malice, and assists our Love" could never have been written by Otway, whose bawd Fortune is a recurring image throughout his work.[35] And most unusual of all, the tragedy resolves happily, with reunited lovers and friends. As Professor Ham commented, "It was all the baldest hoax, and would not be serving of notice, if it did not bear witness to the magic of Otway's name."[36]

This magic apparently touched and transformed many of the tales of Otway's last works and deeds, revealing a sort of wish-fulfillment on the part of the biographers. From this point on, we shall be examining these rather questionable materials with the ulterior purpose of determining what prompted their invention. The *Heroick Friendship* story grew from a fond belief that a poet's last work must necessarily be his finest. Otway's last play, *The Atheist,* had been a self-confessed and widely acknowledged failure, so in a burst of corrective enthusiasm, not to mention greedy hopes of cashing in on the magic name, some unknown eighteenth-century hack wrote the play to fill the need.

Anthony à Wood, whose *Athenae Oxonienses* is not only fairly sober biography but also is close enough to the poet's own time to be reliable (1692), states that Otway was composing a poem celebrating "the inauguration of K. Jam. 2."[37] *The Pastoral on the Death of His Late Majesty,* a fragment, might have been this poem, and so might *Windsor Castle,* also an elegy on the death of Charles. Wood's account notes the irony of the poet's "leane loyalty preserving," and implies a reproach of the Tory aristocracy for failing to reward the fidelity of an important writer.

Still another "last work" tale advises us that Otway "was a Jovial Companion, and a great Lover of the Bottle, and particularly of Punch; the last thing he made before his death, being an excellent Song of that Liquor."[38] This is the kindliest mention of Otway's alleged fondness for drink, and in the nicest possible way it implies that his intemperance may have contributed to his early death. We recall that in *Les Soupirs de la Grand Britaigne* (1713) is the tart assertion that Otway was "more beholding to Captain Symonds the Vintner, in whose Debt he dy'd £400 than to all his Patrons of Quality."[39] *The Tory-Poets* (1682) makes much of the relationship between Otway's poetry and his liquid inspiration:

But who but Fools would praise dull Ot——ys strains,
Compos'd with little wit and lesser pains;
Whose fiery face doth dart as hot a ray,
As the fierce warmer of a Summers day,
Whose very looks would drive the Fiends away.
He may so painted with the juice of Vines,
Turn his Invectives to the praise of Wines . . .
His verse of Wine stinks worse than bawdy Punk
For he never writes a Verse but when he is drunk.[40]

J. C. Ghosh, the editor of Otway's works (1932) was compelled by this lampoon to comment rather primly upon this matter in a passage entitled "Personal Appearance and Character:"

With regard to this aspect of his character I neither make any apologies for him nor try to justify him. An understanding of the age he lived in will extenuate much. For the rest, his life was his own. Also, there is reason to believe that his thwarted passion for Mrs. Barry was to some extent responsible for it.[41]

Having carefully refused to "justify," Ghosh offers part of Otway's letter to Mrs. Barry as evidence of his affliction: "With Stubborn Sufferance, I resolv'd to bear and brave your Power; nay, did it often too, successfully. Generally with Wine or Conversation I diverted or appeas'd the Daemon that possess'd me."[42] By 1738, fifty-three years after his death, Otway was well established in the popular imagination as a dissolute young man. He is described in a fantasy appearing in the *Gentleman's Magazine* of that year:

A Young Man of a divine Aspect appeared and, to my great Amazement, went up to Shadwell in a familiar manner. My Amazement was changed to the utmost Concern, when I saw him affect the same Airs and Motions with him: But there was a remarkable Difference betwixt them, for that abandoned Deportment seemed as unnatural in him, as the Airs of Wit and Politeness appeared in the other. . . . That divine young Man, said my Conductor, is the incomparable Otway, his Genius entitled him to a Place in the first Rank of Men, but the Habits he contracted, threw him into the lowest. Heavens, said I to myself, that a Man who could command the Passions of others should be so great a Slave to his own!"[43]

Thus was another literary legend established—Otway the slave of low habits.

Death Legends

The accounts of Otway's death are all so remote from being firsthand as to be virtually unacceptable, but as reflections of the deep human need to give form and shape to life, according to the moral and aesthetic principles of the time, they are a form of art. Anthony à Wood's version in *Athenae Oxonienses* is the simplest:

At length, after he had lived about 33 years in this vain and transitory world, made his last exit in an house on Tower-hill (called the Bull as I have heard) upon the 14. of Apr. in sixteen hundred eighty and five: whereupon his body was conveyed to the Church of S. Clement Danes within the liberty of Westminster, and was buried in a vault there.[44]

William Oldys was a somewhat later biographer who, among other things, collected the reminiscences of elderly gentlemen who recalled the Restoration theater. His contribution to the tale of Otway's death was to call the Bull not a tavern but a "sponging-house"—that is, a residence kept by the sheriff or bailiff as a preliminary place of confinement for debtors.[45]

John Dennis in 1717 wrote that "Otway died in an alehouse, unpitied, unlamented," but blamed his death upon a fever:

Otway had an intimate friend (one Blackstone) who was shot; the murderer fled toward Dover; and Otway pursued him. In his return, he drank water when violently heated, and so got a fever, which was the death of him.[46]

This story was accepted by Dr. Johnson and elaborated upon by Warton, who had Otway pursuing the murderer to Dover on foot, so deeply was he aggrieved by his friend's murder.[47] Contemporary biographers generally reject the overheated-pursuit theory of Otway's last illness, since Blackstone (or Blakiston) was killed a full year before the poet's death. Professor Ham, however, sees no reason to discredit the tale of the pursuit, although any connection with his death is probably remote at best.

In 1753, Theophilus Cibber embroidered the account of Otway's last minutes, spent in a coffeehouse and not an alehouse, by blending all the elements of poverty, pride, paradox, and excessive sentiment to create an unsurpassed fiction in which the poet's unhappy circumstances become material for moralizing and pity.

After suffering many eclipses of fortune, and being exposed to the most cruel necessities, poor Otway died of want, in a public house on Tower Hill, in the 33rd year of his age, 1685. He had, no doubt, been driven to that part of town, to avoid the persecution of his creditors, and as he durst not appear much abroad to sollicit assistance, and having no means of getting money in his obscure retreat, he perished.

This much is fairly conservative conjecture, based upon Otway's reputation and early reports, but Cibber continues with a tale beginning vaguely, "It has been reported."

Mr. Otway, whom delicacy had long deterred from borrowing small sums, driven at last to the most grievous necessity ventured out of his lurking place, almost naked and shivering, and went into a coffee house on Tower Hill where he saw a gentleman, of whom he had some knowledge, and of whom he solicited the loan of a shilling. The gentleman was quite shocked to see the author of *Venice Preserv'd* begging bread, and compassionately put into his hand a guinea. Mr. Otway having thanked his benefactor, retired, and changed the guinea to purchase a roll; as his stomach was full of wind by excess of fasting, the first mouthful choked him, and instantaneously put a period to his days. [48]

From "delicacy" to "lurking" and "shivering" and on to "instantaneous" death, Cibber's account has the feverish quality of cheap fiction. In his *Lives of the Poets,* Samuel Johnson accepted the idea that Otway had been "hunted as is supposed, by the terriers of the law," but of the choking tale he simply said, "All this, I hope, is not true."[49] We only know that Otway died as he had lived when his Fortune deserted him, "helpless, friendless, very proud, and poor," but his plays lived and thrived long after him.

The Poet of the Passions

The key to the fate of Otway's literary reputation may be found in Dryden's respectful praise of *Venice Preserv'd*:

To express the passions which are seated in the heart, by outward signs, is one great precept of the painters, and very difficult to perform. In poetry, the same passion and motions of the mind are to be express'd: and in this consists the principal difficulty, as well as the excellency of that art . . . not to be obtain'd by pains or study, if we are not born to it; for the motions which are studied, are never so natural as those which break out in the height of a real Passion. Mr. Otway possessed this part as thoroughly as any of the Ancients or Moderns.[50]

Restoration tragedy is deeply preoccupied with psychological portraiture, so that "the moving of the passions" is vitally important. Dryden believed that portrayal of emotion could not be studied or learned, but was an instinctive talent. Dryden's heroic drama shows his own deep interest in Hobbesian and Cartesian passion psychology, which examines the relationship of the passions to the reason. The "passions and motions of the mind" to which he refers concern the psychological process of "suffering a passion" or experiencing an emotion (like jealousy or fear or reverence), then testing the moral validity of the vital physical response to that emotion by applying "right reason" to the selection of responsive action. Dryden's own *All for Love, or the World Well Lost* reveals in its very title the conflict and resolution of his heroine's passions. Reason was believed to be a liberating force in the soul, while the passions could enslave, and so the depiction of the struggle of passions with reason is basically the drama of a struggle for freedom. Reason alone could lead the soul to its most divine motions, while the uninformed, impassioned soul had the potential to degrade and devastate its possessor. Choosing love and renouncing honor—or conversely, forsaking love in favor of honor—illustrates a favorite Restoration tragic dilemma and reveals a profound fascination with extreme psychological states. The hero or heroine who becomes "passion's slave" is surefire box-office. On the other side of the psychological issue, and possibly even more popular, is the martyr figure who is acted upon and often victimized by an impassioned person.

"I will not defend everything in his *Venice Preserv'd*; but I must bear this testimony to his memory, that the passions are truly touch'd in it, though perhaps there is somewhat to be desir'd, both in the grounds of them, and in the height and elegance of expression; but nature is there, which is the greatest beauty."[51] Despite his critical reservations and rational aesthetic judgments, Dryen's praise in this passage foreshadows the taste for the "free" and "natural" flowing of sentiment which characterizes eighteenth and early nineteenth century drama.

William Hazlitt (1778–1830), in his famous criticism of Otway's *The Orphan,* demonstrates the struggle within himself between reason and feeling. First he attacks the play for lacking masculinity, "fortitude," and a heroic quality:

In *The Orphan,* there is little else but this voluptuous effeminacy of sentiment and mawkish distress, which strikes directly at the root of that mental fortitude and heroick cast of thought which alone makes tragedy endurable—that renders its suffering pathetic, or its struggles sublime.

Then rather surprisingly after this wholesale denunciation, he promptly confesses his personal vulnerability to the play:

Yet there are lines and passages in it of extreme tenderness and beauty; and few persons, I conceive (judging from my own experience) will read it at a certain time of life without shedding tears over it as fast as the "Arabian trees their medicinal gums."

From this admission, Hazlitt then takes the step which so many other critics have found irresistible, and draws a portrait of the man based on his reaction to the work:

Otway always touched the reader, for he had himself a heart. We may be sure that he blotted his page often with his tears, on which so many drops have since fallen from glistening eyes, "that sacred pity had engendered there." He had susceptibility of feeling and warmth of genius. . . .

At this point, just as Dryden had felt obliged to "not defend everything," Hazlitt turns on the weeping playwright he has just invented and reproaches him for lack of control, which seems paradoxical to say the least:

. . . but he had not equal depth of thought or loftiness of imagination, and indulged his mere sensibility too much, yielding to the immediate expression of emotion excited in his own mind, and not placing himself enough in the minds and situations of others, or following the workings of nature sufficiently with keenness of eye and strength of will into its heights and depths, its strongholds as well as its weak sides.[52]

What Hazlitt seems to be criticizing as much as the play itself is his own weakness for it: he is ashamed of being moved by what he perceives to be effeminacy of sentiment, and so he condemns Otway for lacking loftiness, depth, and strength.

Otway and the Critics

Criticism invariably tells us as much about the critic—his personal prejudices and the general concerns and tastes of his day, as it does about the work he criticizes. Hazlitt is not the first critic to empathize in this love-hate fashion with the author of a work which stirred him. Indeed, the response of reader to author—person to person—was considered an essential part of the appreciation of a work of literature for many years, and only fairly recently has "biographical criticism" been deemed to be separable from textual criticism.

We must not, therefore, be surprised or offended by twentieth-century critics who searched Otway's works for clues to the poet's own emotional experiences. One of these is the Reverend Montague Summers, who in 1926 brought out an edition of Otway's plays, prefaced by a hundred-page biographical and critical introduction which places Otway in the Restoration theatrical scene with great vividness. Summers, as both literary scholar and genuine "fan" of Restoration theater, is fairly careful to rely upon historical evidence as the basis for his biography. When he "empathizes" with the poet, as he does fairly often, he usually bases his speculation upon his intimate knowledge of the theater and a valid document, as in the case of Downes's brief account of Otway's stage fright. This is the manner in which Summers makes a moment "vivid":

But Otway with parched throat and trembling limbs found himself unable to articulate the words. His glazing eyes saw as through a mist the candle-lit theatre, tier upon tier of faces, the fine ladies, brave in silk and satin, sparkling with gems, that lined the boxes, the gallants leaning over them to pay compliment and pretty speech . . . the young blades in the pit fooling with saucy orange-girls and their dear covey the sharp-tongued black-vizored whores. The sweat poured down from his forehead. He well-nigh swooned, and his failure was complete. . . . So public a catastrophe seemed without any hope of redress, and he may well have thought that the door to that enchanted land for which his heart so yearned was shut fast in his face forever.[53]

We have already noted that Summers presumes too freely upon the character of Mrs. Barry by calling her "hard as adamant, and possibly sexless . . . the perfect whore."[54] In the Barry affair, Summers also explains the poet's feelings of rejection fulsomely:

The wretched poor heart-broken poet was held in captivity, realizing the hopelessness of his love, never able to break his chain. And so in debauchery and intemperance he made shift to forget his despair.[55]

But there are advantages to being as steeped as Summers is in the witty and scurrilous gossip of the theatrical crowd. In defending the artistic integrity of the flagellation scene in *Venice Preserv'd,* Summers unearths a late eighteenth-century critic who subscribed to the theory that Otway was the "slave of low habits:"

It [flagellation] was very well known in the incontinent reign of Charles the Second, and in a comedy of Shadwell's called The Virtuoso, there is a courtesan with a rod going to castigate a gentleman of this order before the audience, but is happily prevented by the introduction of another person. It was supposed, in many of the writings of that day, that Otway was the very person thus satirized, and in one of the many thousand political squibs published at that time in which this great writer flourished the following distich appears:

> Tom Otway loves birch in his heart, and Nat Lee
> With a rod and his Chloris will ever agree.[56]

We must note, in all fairness, that the Reverend Summers is the most open-minded of all of Otway's critics and biographers concerning the sexuality in the plays. Passing on century-old gossip about century-old gossip is, frankly, a literary sport, and as long as its validity is properly questioned (as it is not in *Fashionable Lectures* of 1785), it has its place. Summers is on more doubtful territory when he meditates personally upon Otway's character: "he was self-indulgent; a fault, no doubt, yet a fault for which he answered very dearly, and 'tis but a sick morality which continues to condemn the sin for which the sinner has paid the price."

It is very interesting to study the extent to which critics of the 1920s and early 1930s dwelled upon the implications of Otway's six love-letters and freely blamed the actress for his early death. Summers says that Mrs. Barry was "a cool, calculating whore, with whom love was an auction not an emotion. Such an infatuation might wreck any man's career."[57] In 1929, Bonamy Dobree's study "Thomas Otway" picks up this thread:

Unable or unwilling to forbid approaches, she kept the unfortunate Otway in a state of suspense which drove him to distraction. This was the central experience which determined his outlook and his mentality; it made him the poet he was, though in destroying the man it may have stifled a still greater poet.[58]

Dobree therefore, instead of discussing the notorious flagellation scene, chooses Jaffeir's admission of betrayal from *Venice Preserv'd* and observes that Otway "was exploring not man's courage so much as his capacity for feeling, even for self-torture. Jaffeir's remorse and self-abasement are terrible to listen to; Otway seems to be indulging in a debauch of his own pains."[59]

Professor Roswell Gray Ham, in his double biography *Otway and Lee: Portrait of an Age* (1930), discovered some new records and pursued the Blackstone murder story, thereby contributing significantly to the factual knowledge concerning the poet. Yet even he espouses the love-ruined artist theory. Contemplating the Faithorne engraving which reproduces the Soest portrait, Ham looks into the poet's eyes and allows himself this empathetic musing:

Such he was in his thirtieth year, a figure of ineffectual protest, the lines of discontent prematurely furrowed upon his brow and about his mouth, his cheek and jowl inclined to flabbiness, the whole man ill conditioned to play his part in any sort of tragedy.[60]

Even the most recent critics of Otway, therefore, have perpetuated a literary legend of softness, self-indulgence, self-pity, and debauchery which cannot be justified in light of the meager evidence available. Of all of these, only Aline Mackenzie Taylor sensibly refuses to delineate Otway's character. In her *Next to Shakespeare,* she points out that the reputation of his works and the interest in the Otway legends rise and fall in tandem over the centuries. Her own fine study of *Venice Preserv'd* focuses upon the importance of personal relationships in the tragedy. Perhaps this personal element is the key to the legend-factory: from Dryden on, critics have not been able to read Otway without feeling themselves irresistibly drawn in to the plays. Thus they have found the tragedies exquisitely natural or effeminately mawkish, according to how they themselves respond emotionally. They may be shocked into speechlessness or nauseated by the sexuality of the comedies or the "Nicky-Nacky" flagellation scene. They assume that Otway was the gentlest, the most victimized, the most disillusioned, or even the most depraved dramatic writer of the Restoration.

Yet the distortion of Otway's biography does illustrate the extraordinary and very special power of his dramatic gift. Where critical involvement may have led to unjustifiable bursts of empathy or disgust with the author, it has also led to valuable insights into the plays. Summers, Dobree, Ham, and Ghosh have taken what earlier critics called "tenderness," for example, and found a complex of emotions that they do not label "masochism" as such, but which brought together portray a realm of human experience which Otway was especially skilled at portraying. Abasement, remorse, shame, self-pity, and self-disgust, as well as degradation, are all a part of this complex of suffering which Otway depicts so fully and feelingly that critics either flinch at the unmanliness of it or find it a vehicle for the liberation of the deepest natural passions. Otway's readers have been unfair to the author, but it can never be said that they have been indifferent to his work.

Chapter Two
Otway's View of the Political Scene (1679–1683)

Emerging Political Awareness

We have seen that there was a good deal of interest in the personal details of Otway's life, yet comparatively little attention has been paid him as a critic and observer of the political scene. In this chapter we will deal selectively with this side of the poet's work, in order to present his view of the series of social and political crises of the Restoration.

The Poet's Complaint of His Muse is autobiographical to the point at which Reason lifts "the veil of Dotage" from the Bard's eyes and shows him his Muse as she truly is, "a rampant, tawdry Quean." The last figure in her degenerate train of flatterers is "a Beest of Monstrous guise . . . and Libell was his name." More than half of this poem, from this moment on, is political satire directed against the evils of Libell and his mother, "the Good Old Cause" of the Cromwell Protestants: it is plain that Otway's purpose is to show that his own misfortunes as an artist are the result of the political convulsions which followed upon the Popish Plot crisis.

But this poem is not the only timely political comment Otway delivers. His prologues and epilogues, his imposition of a scene of full-fledged rebellion upon the story of Romeo and Juliet, his caricatures of the Whig bourgeoisie in his three original comedies, and the all-pervasive tension and explosiveness of the situation in *Venice Preserv'd*—all these are consciously written topical polemics revealing a deep sense of the nation's instability as seen from a Tory viewpoint.

Caius Marius

Otway had been away from England in the winter of 1678–79 when Titus Oates was busy making his hysterical accusations of Catholic treason. When he returned in 1679, the trials were underway, and his profound shock at the state of affairs is immediately reflected in his work. *Caius Marius* (August 1679) features a bloodthirsty mob and swindling politicians who will bribe and kill in order to maintain their political positions. The allegorical half of *The Poet's Complaint,* published in 1680, is Otway's most thorough analysis of the alarming civil turbulence of that season. *The Soldier's Fortune* (1680) portrays middle-class rebels, greedy for land and preferments, as well as dangerous city streets teeming with hired ruffians. Each of these reflects the stages in his thinking which lead him to the violent ambivalence of his acknowledged masterpiece, *Venice Preserv'd.*

In the course of this one highly productive season Otway became a full-fledged satirist, although in the Prologue to *The Orphan* he explains his distaste for satire:

> Satyr's the effect of Poetries disease;
> Which, sick of a lew'd Age, she vents for Ease.

In this prologue he boasts that he has never stooped to character assassination, though only a few months earlier in *The Poet's Complaint* he had vilified Lord Shaftesbury, the leader of the Whigs in Parliament, without mercy. Lord Shaftesbury and the old Presbyterian witch produce the offspring Libell, who takes after his father in appearance:

> The nose was ugly, long and big,
> Broad and snowty, like a Pig;
> Which shew'd he would in Dunghills love to dig . . .

Otway's portraits of the Whig Green-Ribbon men, and Shaftesbury in particular, become increasingly vicious after this as he sees the enemies of art to be synonymous with the enemies of peace and honor.

It is with *Caius Marius* that Otway first shows his interest in contemporary politics. His first two tragedies, *Alcibiades* (1675) and *Don Carlos* (1676), merely portrayed kings faced with problems within their courts—disloyal queens, evilly scheming advisers, problem sons—who were undone by their own human weaknesses, such as susceptibility to flattery or sexual jealousy. But in *Caius Marius* we suddenly find an original and politically relevant secondary plot running beside the frankly plagiarized love story of Romeo and Juliet, known here as Marius Junior and Lavinia.

Old Marius, the heart of the subplot, is modeled after Lord Shaftesbury even to the point of being described as "consum'd with Age, and by Diseases prest." When Shaftesbury assumed office in 1679, he announced that he intended to serve the country as the "Tribune of the People," and reassured his supporters that he would continue to be the champion of the "average" (Whig) man. Old Marius makes much of his humble birth as evidence of his concern for the common people in his deeply hypocritical public speeches. Through military conquests abroad, use of force and terror at home, and outright bribery of the voting citizens, Marius Senior has acquired vast power, served six times as consul of Rome, and at the moment of the play's beginning is scheming to force himself into the consulship again by his usual violent methods. Otway found in Plutarch's life of Caius Marius a number of incidents which, in his opinion, could be construed as parallels to his own time.

One of these is the outrageous abuse of election procedure which throughout the 1670s had been perpetrated by wealthy and noble Whigs. One of Charles's first acts after the Restoration had been to reform the boroughs in order to give more influence to the country nobility. This proved to be a mistake. It was expected that the country gentry would support the crown as they always had, but the king's brother and successor James managed to alienate them so thoroughly that borough reform worked instead to intensify court opposition.[1]

In the Norfolk election of 1675, for example, the Whig Lord Townshend contrived to send his candidate to Parliament through the calculated ploy of neglecting to write poll-watchers into the election regulations. Townshend's voters knew that they could vote as many times as they pleased, while the opponent's supporters were slow to observe the ruse. When at last somebody caught Whig voters lining up over and over again, the regulations were examined and officially found to lack a provision for poll-watchers. So the court voters joined in the fray, voting as often and as fast as they could in a race to the deadline. The Whigs had had the advantage of time and so Townshend's party won.[2]

There were even more preposterous violations of procedure. David Ogg reports another recorded case, in Abingdon, where the electorate rallied to vote a majority to the candidate opposed by the Tory nobility 297 to 171. After a private conference, the mayor announced to the city corporation that "he had examined the poll and found 171 was greater than 297."[3] But by far the easiest and most common method of purchasing votes was through gifts of liquor and food. Parliamentary legislation of 1677 attempted to limit the value of such "gifts" to ten pounds' worth per voter, which still seems an extravagant sum.

Old Marius was such a strategist. Otway clearly blames the "giddy Multitude" for selling its franchise to the most generous candidate, "Never consulting who 'tis best deserves, / But who Feasts highest to obtain their Suffrage." At the last moment before the election, old Marius personally wheels in "a mighty vessel of Falernian Wine" to the Forum:

> Then when a while he had
> With a smooth tale tickled their Asses Ears,
> H'at both ends tapp'd his Butt, and got the
>   Consulship.

It is not difficult to understand why elections during the Exclusion Crisis were frequently the occasion for bloody riots, for this practice of "treating" the voters was hardly conducive to promoting civil order.[4]

Old Marius is aided by his young henchman Sulpitius, a well-born soldier commanding an unscrupulous brigade of six hundred Roman youths who terrorize the city by night. Sulpitius might be analogous to the Duke of Monmouth, Charles's illegitimate son and "the Protestant hope," while the young ruffians are surely the Whig toughs who were frightening Londoners off the streets at night all through 1679. Fear of a militia was not limited to the king's party, however, for Charles had tenaciously held on to his army and the Green Ribbon men for their part were increasingly fearful of its possible retaliatory uses, particularly in the event of James's succession.

Metellus, Lavinia's father, is a senator who has suffered through the corruption of Marius's six terms of office and would rather die than see him in power again. Old Marius's proposal of a marriage between his son and Lavinia is nothing more than a cheap attempt to purchase a coalition with the faction of the Senate which has turned against him. The two men address a crowd outside the Forum in the second act of

Caius Marius, and here we see a bit of Whig and Tory street politics through Otway's eyes. The gullible citizens believe that Marius must be on their side because he is not an aristocrat. They particularly relish defending him in brawls, for as one of them says, "There's nothing like a Civil Government, where good subjects may have leave to knock Brains out to maintain Privileges."

Marius addresses the crowd first, boasting of his creation of a party in the Senate in their behalf which will help them to resist "the hard yoak of Lordly pow'r." He claims to be the protector of the hard-won rights and laws favoring free-born men, and he points to "these Wounds, which in your Service I have got." The crowd shouts, "Marius! Marius! Marius! No Sylla, no Sylla, no Sylla."

Representing the opposition, Metellus addresses them next and warns them of Marius's ambition to seize their property and their rights and enslave them. Here again Otway touches a nerve with a subject which frightened both Whigs and Tories. The landed Tories were alarmed by Whig uprisings in the boroughs, and quite legitimately dreaded the possibility of a middle-class revolt. The Whig gentry, on their side, worried that if a Catholic king were to reclaim the church property which had become theirs in the time of Henry VIII, they would be totally ruined. But the crowd in the play responds to this last warning with preposterous fickleness and chants, "No Marius! No Marius! No Marius!"

At this point Marius gives the order to "dam the Rabble, let 'em fall / Like common Dross. . . ." Sulpitius kills the consul's son, a bloody brawl ensues, and Marius's faction triumphs by force as the crowd disperses in panic. Then the old politician expresses his true contempt for the people:

> These wide-mouth'd Brutes that bellow thus for
>   Freedome,
> Oh! how they ran before the hand of Pow'r,
> Flying for shelter into every Brake!
> Like cowardly fearful Sheep they break their
>   Herd,
> When the Wolf's out, and ranging for his Prey.

Later in the play, the "triumphal" return of Marius to Rome following a period of exile is a hellish scene of bloody slaughter. We see the tyrant ordering the rape of all Roman virgins and the butchering of all old men and children. This passage, in its hysteria, is worthy of the author of the anonymous Whig propaganda pamphlet, *An Appeal from the Country to the City*. Though the condemned plead piteously for the privilege of sacrificing themselves to the gods in order to save the rest of the populace, Marius jeeringly turns them down:

> Who trusts your Penitence is more than Fool.
> Rebellion will renew: ye can't be honest.
> Y'are never pleas'd but with the Knaves that
>   cheat you,
> And work your Follies to their private ends.
> For your Religion, like your Cloaths you wear it,
> To change and turn just as the Fashion alters.

The chief interest in *Caius Marius* lies in its demonstration of Otway's newly emerged political awareness and apprehensions including his dread of another Cromwell regime, its sharp warning to the unthinking, bribable English voter, and a firm belief that art can flourish only under a stable government.

The Poet's Complaint and the Exclusion Crisis

Otway's next critique of the current political scene is found in the allegorical biography of Libell in *The Poet's Complaint*. Libell's mother is a witch and a whore, the spirit of the Civil War, who has returned to London to practice her profession in the year of the fire and the plague, 1665. Her clients include a collection of variously disgruntled bourgeois who hope to "thrive by the Distractions of a nation."

Otway saw these "distractions" in terms of the Popish Plot, for the violence and dissension of 1679 were fueled by the allegations made during this furor. Titus Oates, the instigator of the rumor of the Plot, claimed that he had learned during his time in an English Jesuit college that King Charles was considered to be an obstacle to the conversion of England, and so plans were afoot among the Jesuits to remove him and thus see the Catholic James safely to the throne. The story was elaborated upon as further "revelations" came to Oates. He claimed to have found out that Popish conspirators were planning to raze the city of

London, and bring in a military force of Irish Catholics which, with the aid of French troops, would then conquer England, murder all Protestants who refused to convert, and finally murder the king. Word of the Popish Plot spread like wildfire.

Oates and a writer friend, Doctor Israel Tonge, filed their papers with a London judge, Sir Edmund Berry Godfrey, who had agreed to publish them if the court tried to stifle the news of the Plot. Godfrey informed the Duke of York's secretary, Coleman, of this arrangement, and not long after his disclosure he was found murdered in a ditch near Primrose Hill. Coleman was then arrested, and a search of his residence produced what was described as "treasonable correspondence" with Louis XIV's confessor and with the Papal nuncio.[5] Godfrey was therefore popularly believed to be the first victim of the Popish conspiracy. Four days after the murder Parliament passed a unanimous resolution asserting its belief in the existence of a Plot: Charles was forced into requiring the immediate imprisonment of all Catholics, summoning the militia, and placing cannon all around his palace.

Coleman's correspondence was found to express hopes that Protestantism might be overthrown in England and requests for financial assistance to Charles from Louis so that he might be free of his dependence upon Parliament. The letters were real enough, but the alarm they produced led to unreasonable arrests, trials, and convictions of a great many innocent people.

Titus Oates was a relentless witch-hunter, intoxicated with the importance and attention his charges had given him, and he strove to maintain his position in the limelight. He brought charges against Jesuits and Benedictines for plotting against the king's person. Eventually, he even charged that it had been "revealed" to him that the queen's own physician was a potential assassin. In his fine history *England Under Charles the Second,* David Ogg describes the turbulence:

Round Oates there surged a broth, all the ingredients of which had the same characteristic flavor. Incriminating letters were found behind wainscots or at the bottom of tubs; concocted papers were "planted" on victims and then searched for; accused persons turned informers, and victimized others: the families of the arch-informers took up the prosperous trade of papist-hunting, or made money by informing against their own relatives; confessions were recanted and again sworn to; both truth and honor were completely dissolved in this boiling mass.[6]

When Otway returned from Flanders in August 1679, discord was at its peak. The Duke of Monmouth, Charles's illegitimate son, had just quelled a rebellion at Bothwell Brig and had become such a popular military figure that some feared the possibility of another Cromwellian takeover. James had been dispatched to Brussels in order that the violent emotions surrounding the idea of his succession might subside with his absence.

At the time of the first performance of *Caius Marius,* however, James had just secretly returned to England to be at his brother's bedside, for Charles was suddenly and gravely ill and was expected to die. It is generally agreed that if he had died at this time, civil war would almost certainly have begun. The illness had heightened tensions by making the Tories more fully aware of their vulnerability and the Whigs more sensible of their strength. By the time James had surreptitiously made his way to Windsor, Charles had survived the crisis in his fever thanks to a new medicine, quinine, which was popularly known at the time as Jesuit's powder.[7] After a decent time James was persuaded to go off again, this time to Scotland, and Monmouth was summarily relieved of his command and given a post in Holland. But London, the stronghold of the Whigs, was anything but calm after these events: city leaders had been prepared during the king's illness to proclaim Monmouth's legitimacy and support his cause, and Whig spirits were still high.

Inevitably the events of September through December 1679 terrified the Tories as well as anyone who merely longed for civil tranquility. The murder of Godfrey was followed by a Pope-burning procession and then widespread rioting; and after Monmouth's unannounced return to England from Holland, bonfires were lighted all over London to express support for his presence. Even when panic subsided, fear prevailed for years afterward and fueled the energetic efforts in behalf of excluding James from succession to the throne.

In *The Poet's Complaint* we see the Presbyterian whore feigning piety and humility to attract the business of "all those who use Religion for a Fashion, / All such as practise Forms, and take great pains / To make their Godliness their Gains."

> Nay, to her side at last she drew in all
>   the rude,
> Ungovernable, headlong Multitude:
> Promis'd strange Liberties, and sure Redress

> Of never-felt, unheard-of Grievances;
> Pamper'd their Follies, and indulg'd their
>   Hopes,
> With May-day Routs, November-Squibs, and
>   burning Pastboard Popes.

"May-day Routs" alludes to the celebration which the Whigs prepared annually upon the date of the king's restoration, May 29. These festivities had become so disruptive of the peace that by 1680 Charles found it necessary to issue an order forbidding any public commemoration of this event by presuming "to make or encourage the making of any Bonfires or other publick Fireworks on the Twenty-ninth day of May next ensuing."[8]

On November 17, the official birthday of Queen Elizabeth, the Protestant Whigs rallied for their cause. Thanks to Oates and his charges of Catholic plotting, "Pope-burning" was a feature of the birthday procession, and the spectacle of 1679 to which Otway alludes was the largest political demonstration against Popery to date. In the procession appeared a dummy representing Sir Edmund Berry Godfrey, the murdered judge: this ghoulish apparition shows the extent of Whig use of street theater, and the fact that between 150,000 and 200,000 people were in attendance suggests the intensity of public involvement in the Exclusion issue. The dummy was described by Otway later in his prologue to *Venice Preserv'd:*

> Here's not one murther'd Magistrate at least,
> Kept rank like Ven'son for a City feast,
> Grown four days stiff, the better to prepare
> And fit his plyant limbs to ride in Chair.

Godfrey's dummy was followed by mock Jesuits "freely" giving pardons, four "Popish bishops in purple," and others, concluding with the dummy of the Pope, which was to be burned, "preceded by silk banners with bloody daggers painted on them for murdering heretical kings, and behind him his counsellor the Devil."[9] It is with such divertisements that Otway's Witch, the Good Old Cause, keeps alive the hopes of her disreputable admirers.

Religious toleration, the sanctity of private property, and personal liberty constituted the three essential planks of the Whig platform at this time, for as Ogg points out, the Whigs "included a considerable proportion of both the landed nobility and the landed gentry, as well as many rich city merchants and rich Dissenters. From these constituent elements can be deduced two of their fundamental principles—sanctity of private property and religious toleration."[10] From Otway's point of view, "Through her the Atheist hop'd to purchase Toleration, / The Rebell Pow'r, the beggar'd Spendthrift Lands, / Out of the Kings or Bishop's hands."

The Exclusion crisis was a single-issue situation—prevent James from succeeding his brother—and it is important to understand why the Duke of York was so widely feared. J. L. Jones in *The First Whigs* cites two reasons: James's advocacy of repression made him seem a tyrannical character, and his conversion to Catholicism was publicly acknowledged.[11] Great numbers of Englishmen found it possible to align themselves with Shaftesbury and the Whigs in their opposition, although they disagreed widely on constructive solutions to the problem of succession. Because of the concentrated support of such a large portion of the population, and because of the expiration of the Licensing Act of 1662 at that time, the Whig propaganda machine was for a time unbridled in its attacks on the court, on James in particular, and on Papists in general. Shaftesbury asserted that "Popery and arbitrary government were sisters going hand in hand."[12] James was expected to establish a military dictatorship if he succeeded, undoing the constitution altogether. It was then believed necessary to use every expedient to push through the Exclusion Bill before it was too late. Following the king's illness, awareness that James was so close to the throne heightened the intensity of exclusion efforts.

Since subsequent generations bring their own prejudices and hindsight to the reading of history, interpretations of the Exclusion Crisis are, with few exceptions, favorable to the Whigs. Seen as striking blow after blow for parliamentary government, religious toleration, and civil liberties, the early Whigs have been transformed into heroes of democracy, visionaries of a better society, poets of freedom. Understanding Otway's contempt for these brave democrats, then, is a bit difficult at first. It is an interesting exercise, however, to read his lines describing the education of Libell with the rich scorn their author intended. Libell's tutors,

> Distinguisht to him in an Hour
> 'Twixt Legislative and Judicial Power;
> How to frame a Commonwealth,
> And Democracy, by stealth;
> To palliate it at first, and Cry
> 'Twas but a Well-mixt Monarchy
> And Treason Salus Populi . . .

For his education Libell is sent to Scotland, where Presbyterianism thrives, and there he studies "old worn-out Statutes and Records / Of Commons Privileges, and the Rights of Lords." Whig propagandists were particularly skillful in citing ancient legal precedents to suit their purposes. Libell also becomes, under Presbyterian tutelage, an adept in the art of pious hypocrisy:

> T'ave no Religion, Honesty or Sense
> But to profess them all for a Pretense.

We must keep in mind that in the heat of the moment, the Whigs were often ruthless and reprehensible in their tactics. They drew up petitions signed by people not legally qualified to vote, they created hundreds of freemen, they interfered at the polls. While some of their campaign strategies have become common practice, many others disgrace the ideal of democracy. They bribed voters, stuffed ballot boxes, and accepted large sums of money from Louis XIV, their avowed enemy, an absolute monarch and a Papist, whose power over the Stuarts they claimed to dread and despise. They accused their opponents of crooked deals which they themselves had originated, and above all they maintained a sanctimonious front. Says Jones, "The Whigs were hypocritical and practical: their purpose was to eliminate opponents and at the same time gain a reputation for virtue."[13]

Despite the efforts of Whig historians to argue otherwise, their purpose in 1680 was not part of a far-ranging political vision as much as it was the single expedient of displacing James as successor. Toward this end they hired mobs, burned effigies, terrified people with tales of assassination plots and conspiracies, and generally made themselves visible and audible. Otway's Libell is a typical Whig orator:

Where-ere he came, 'twas he first silence broke,
And swell'd with every Word he spoke:
. . . By many for Preferments was thought fit,
For talking Treason without Fear or Wit:
For opening Failings in the State;
For loving noisie and unsound Debate,
And wearing of a Mysticall green Ribband in his
    Hat.

Propaganda and Perjury

Libell personifies in Otway's mind the two evils of propaganda and perjury. Propaganda was everywhere in 1680: the Whig press was essential to the Exclusion cause for exchanging news and information between the city and the country.[14] The petitioning for a Parliament required nationwide dissemination of voter information (and Whig opinion), emphasizing the importance of the elections and of unification of sentiment against James. The Licensing Act of 1662 had forbidden publication of any document contradicting the principles of Christianity or the Church of England, or "tending to the scandal of government or governors in church or state."[15] Roger L'Estrange had been appointed in 1663 as one of the king's licensers, and he promptly classified those seditious opinions which would require suppression. But in May 1679, the month in which the Habeas Corpus Act was passed, the Licensing Act of 1662 expired, and the largely Whig Parliament intentionally failed to renew or replace it. Said Bulstrode in his memoirs, "There came out every day such swarms of impudent licentious libels upon all sorts of persons, and upon all subjects, printed, as the like was never known, and will be still continued whilst the Habeas Corpus is still in force, and that they are sure to be bailed."[16] At last the king was obliged to replace the Licensing Act with a royal proclamation, issued on Halloween of 1679, requiring the seizure of libelous publications and the arrest of their authors and publishers. This somewhat subdued Whig propaganda during the months that Parliament was prorogued, but when a new session began in October a year later, publication was put firmly under the protection of the House of Commons.

Otway surprises Libell in the arms of "my faithless Clio." Now a propagandist, he is bedecked with verses of all kinds, including "Painter's Advices, Letanies, Ballads."

> He was Poetry all o'er,
> On every side, behind, before:
> About him nothing could I see,
> But partycolour'd Poetry.

When Andrew Marvell's *Advice to a Painter,* written originally in 1673 but reprinted in 1679 to fuel the anti-Catholic sentiment of the Plot trials, appeared and captivated the Whig imagination, a number of anonymous works in this genre popped up, including *New Advice to a Painter* and *Second Advice to a Painter:*

> Each puny brother of the rhyming trade
> At every turn implores the Painters Aid,
> And fondly enamour'd of his own foul brat,
> Cries in an ecstacy, Paint this, Draw that!

Even Otway eventually tried his hand at the fashion in his *Windsor Castle,* though this is a Royalist poem in which the poet directs a painter in how to eulogize Charles for posterity upon the ceiling mural at St. George's Chapel at Windsor.

The "Litany" alluded to was a simple form of three rhymed lines of verse followed by the refrain "Libera Nos, Domine." Although a natural vehicle for anti-Catholic sentiment with its Latin refrain, the form was used by Whigs and Tories alike. The Tory Litany of the Duke of Buckingham demonstrates the effects achieved by a scurrilous tercet followed by "Libera Nos."

> From judging the judges in a senseless speech,
> From following Shaftesbury, that wriggling
>   leech,
> Because by turns both f——d the same bitch,
>   Libera Nos.[17]

Also credited to Libell is "that worthy Piece of Modern Wit, / The Countrey's Late Appeal." *An Appeal from the Country to the City for the*

Preservation of His Majesty's Person, Liberty, Property and the Protestant Religion was probably the most notorious of the Whig pamphlets. It alerts Protestants to the Popish peril in the most inflammatory terms, calling on them to envisage "their houses in flames, their children and neighbors massacred, their wives and daughters violated, and their ministers and teachers tortured by the Papists. Let them not be deceived: this imaginary spectacle would be infallibly realized on the succession of a Popish monarch."[18] The pamphlet goes so far as to urge citizens to arm themselves against imminent Papist attack to be perpetrated by "young beggarly officers, courtiers, overhot Churchmen and Papists."[19] It charges further (accurately, as it turns out) that Charles and James are sponsored by French money, and so the Protestant Duke of Monmouth is the only acceptable solution to the problem of succession because "his life depends upon the same bottom with yours." This pamphlet was widely circulated, revealing the strength of the Whig propaganda effort.

There can be no question that during the Popish Plot trials, still going at the time of the writing of *The Poet's Complaint*, Libell in the form of perjury had indeed become a predatory monster stalking the countryside, making "faithfull Servants Traitours." The courts which tried the alleged traitors were by modern standards shockingly unfair to the accused prisoner, who did not even have to be informed until he came into the court what crime he had been charged with. He had no counsel in his defense and such witnesses as he might be able to summon to testify in his behalf were not compelled to appear, nor were they permitted to take the oath. The concurring testimony of two witnesses against him was sufficient to convict him of treason. George Macauley Trevelyan observes, "In a century when the State perpetually feared, and several times suffered, overthrow, the Courts of Law were citadels against treason, rather than asylums for innocence."[20] One can imagine what a prisoner would feel in such a courtroom, being charged with participating in a Catholic conspiracy under such circumstances, knowing that the king was signing death warrants simply to calm popular sentiment. Charles's behavior in this matter was both morally and politically reprehensible, since he knew Titus Oates to be a liar: one may only explain his willingness to sacrifice innocent lives on the grounds of preserving his own life and the monarchy by any politically expedient means. It was not until 1696 that reforms were enacted which offered any real protection to the prisoner in trials for treason. The Habeas Corpus Act had been passed in 1679 during the first Whig Parliament, ensuring that a man charged with treason would at least hear the charges against him in court rather than being summarily imprisoned. But considering the weakness of trial procedure and the king's cooperation with the courts, it is conceivable that thanks to that law, some of the men charged with conspiracy were hastened to their deaths rather than languishing alive in prison until the crisis passed. Another curious fact about the Habeas Corpus Act, revealed by Bishop Burnet, is that it would never have passed had not the House of Lords been in a frivolous mood that day so that the vote of one extremely fat lord was humorously counted as ten.[21]

Last of all Libell attacks the "Royall Brother," whose innocence, courage and purity of character Otway describes elaborately, concluding with a scene of the parting of Charles and James. Otway compares Libell's viciousness to the dragon of ancient legend who was "sent to lay a sinfull Kingdom waste." Ravaging the countryside, despoiling virgins, the dragon at last arrives in London:

> When to the Sacrifice at last
> Th'unhappy Monarch's onely Child must bow:
> A Royal Daughter needs must suffer then, a Royall
> Brother now.

In the tale of St. George, the dragon was just at the point of devouring the princess Sabra who had been offered as a sacrifice by the townspeople, when the saint "slew the dragon and smote of his head" just in the nick of time. Using the analogy as a transition, Otway mourns James's victimization by Whig libels and proceeds to eulogize the royal brother for the next five stanzas.

In order to understand, if not appreciate, the sudden sugary confection of praise which Otway spins around a singularly cold and unlovable individual, we must recollect the vehemence and concentrated force behind the Exclusion effort and view this lavish encomium as an attempt at Tory rebuttal. The acid tone of satire gives way to flattery and querulousness as the poet insists that James's "spotless Fame" is certain to "for ever stand unblemisht" simply because,

> Heaven took such Care
> To make him every thing that's rare,
> Dear to the Heart, desirous to the Eyes.

Citing his naval triumph against the Dutch as evidence of his total dedication to the well-being of England, Otway builds a case for the Duke of York's being a much maligned innocent. "Why lives he in the World's Esteem, / Not one Man's Foe?" One of Otway's moralizing biographers wrote in 1818:

Besides the dissoluteness of manners displayed in his life and writings, he was a shameless flatterer of the great, and seems to have had no other public principle than a servile attachment to authority.[22]

Otway's argument in James's behalf does seem feeble, to say the least. But the Royalists were on the defensive, driven by the relentless attacks of the Whigs almost to the point of swearing fealty to the ideas of absolute monarchy, divine right, and the illegitimacy of petitioning for Parliament. The Stuart historian Trevelyan notes, rather dryly:

If Nero were hereditary King of England, they would let him take their lands, their tithes, their laws, their very lives, without raising a hand against him. The Universities of Oxford and Cambridge, and the Anglican clergy throughout the land, regularly proclaimed these astonishing doctrines.[23]

For the account of the injuries which Libell has inflicted upon the Royal Brothers, Otway abandons the barbed insightfulness of satire and assumes what became known as his "mighty line" of pathos to describe the parting of the two by the Thames outside Whitehall. "A tender Infant in the Nurse's Arms" embraces his "manly Neck," a "sad lamenting Throng" at the shore comes to express "the Pomp of Grief" as James and his wife tearfully board the barge to leave for the "hated Shore." The sentimentality which suffuses this passage avoids, by obfuscation, making a real political observation. Libell has victimized a member of the royal family and oh, the pity of it! When detailing the vices of the Exclusionists, Otway can be mercilessly specific, but here only a perfumed haze of sentiment must take the place of explaining the necessity for loyalty.

The Soldier's Fortune

Turning now to *The Soldier's Fortune,* we find a background of London's city politics in 1680. Charles had contrived, by challenging city charters one by one all over England, to transfer their control to loyalists. London had resisted, refusing to surrender its charter, and its government was in the hands of the Whigs. Sir Davy Dunce, the silly old cuckold in this play, sees his opportunity to advance himself in the new city politics. He is "one of those Fools forsooth, that are led by the Nose by Knaves to rail against the King and the Government, and is mightily fond of being thought of as a party." At one point in the farce, Sir Davy believes that he has been invited to dine with the Lord Mayor, and thus he is duped into leaving Lady Dunce alone with her lover Beaugard. He is transported with delight over the invitation, for he is sure that he is about to become an important person:

Vermin, go get the Coach ready, get me the Gold Medal too and Chain which I took from the Roman Catholik Officer for a Popish Relick: I'l be fine, I'l shine and drink Wine that's Divine, My Lord Mayor invite me to supper!

The changing political climate of 1680 is evident throughout the play. The gallant-heroes are painfully aware that Fortune has turned against them in order to favor the Whigs. It was Fortune, they complain, that brought them back from war and disbanded the troops. In fact, it was the Parliament of 1678 which had required the dissolution of the army. Charles had 30,000 soldiers within summoning distance of English shores, and Whigs and Tories united for the moment in their eagerness to disintegrate this military power, fearing the existence of a secret agreement with France. The soldiers came home to find "Debentures instead of ready Money," and anxiety abated until Louis, unscrupulously capitalizing on the English panic, revealed to the Whigs that there was indeed a secret pact.[24]

Violence in the streets of London accompanied the tension of that winter, and it is reflected in the complaint of the character Bloody-Bones, a professional killer who is losing his livelihood because of the amateur competition:

In peaceable times a man may eat and drink comfortably on't, a private Murder done handsomely is worth Money: but now that the Nation's unsettled, there are so many general undertakers, that 'tis grown almost a Monopoly, you may have a man Murder'd almost for little or nothing and no Body e'r know who did it neither.

In a rather lengthy character sketch in the second act, Otway describes the "new rebel" of 1680. Singling out a "Rogue" with a "busie face," Captain Beaugard tells his story of success and opportunism:

He was born a Vagabond, and no Parish own'd him, his Father was as obscure as his Mother was publick, every body knew her, and no body could guess at him. . . . The first thing he chose to rise by, was Rebellion, so a Rebel he grew, and flourisht a Rebel, fought against his King, and helpt to bring him to the Block. . . . He could pray till he cry'd and preach till he foam'd, which excellent Talent made him popular, and at last prefer'd him to be a worthy Member of that never to be forgotten Rump Parliament. . . .

As in *The Poet's Complaint,* Otway believes that the perpetrators of the Exclusion crisis and the Popish Plot are the same rebels who executed Charles the first and assumed power under the Puritan Oliver Cromwell:

In short, he was Committee man, Sequestrator and Persecutor General of a whole Country, by which he got enough at the Kings Return to secure himself in the general Pardon. . . . Thus forgiven, thus rais'd, and made thus happy, the ungrateful Slave disowns the hand that healed him, cherishes Factions to affront his Master, and once more would Rebel against the Head, which so lately saved his from a Pole.

In a most succinct fashion, this passage enumerates all the Whig characteristics that Otway loathed: the false piety shrouding a merce-nary heart, and the sly bourgeois opportunism which stops at nothing, not even murder, in the pursuit of material aggrandizement.

Venice Preserv'd

Two stormy years passed before Otway's next play appeared, *Venice Preserv'd.* In the interim Charles battled with three successive Whig

Parliaments, proroguing each of them before they had a chance to pass an Exclusion Bill. Finally by the device of requiring that Parliament be held in Oxford, a Tory stronghold where the Whig Members of Parliament were sure to feel threatened by loyalist students, Charles managed to prorogue this parliament as well when it began considering the usual question of succession. He surprised everyone by changing into his robes of state (which he must wear to prorogue Parliament) in the carriage on his way to the assembly.[25] Following this tricky dispersal, the rejoicing in Oxford was so exuberant that the Whigs were obliged to sneak out of town however they could manage. Their terrified flight was considered a Tory triumph. When *Venice Preserv'd* appeared, there was considerable satisfaction that the Whiggish impertinence had at last been subdued by the king's display of political savoir faire, although there were only emotional grounds for believing that the troubles were over. Thus, when the plotters in *Venice Preserv'd* are found out and despatched, the loyal audience interpreted this as a parallel to their own time, though Otway pretends to deny any such analogy in his prologue:

> In these distracted times, when each man dreads
> The bloudy stratagems of busie heads;
> When we have fear'd three years we know not
>   what,
> Till Witnesses begin to die o' the rot,
> What made our Poet meddle with a Plot?
> Was't that he fansy'd for the very sake
> And name of Plot, his trifling Play might
>   take? . . .
> No, of such Tools our Author has no need,
> To make his Plot, or make his Play succeed.

Otway characteristically protests too much in his prologues and epilogues, and just in case anyone might miss them, he points out the intentional parallels—to armed rebels and to Shaftesbury:

> Yet here's an Army rais'd, though under
>   ground,
> But no man seen, nor one Commission found;
> Here is a Traitour too, that's very old,
> Turbulent, subtle, mischievous and bold.

The play is dedicated with customary extravagance to Charles's French mistress, the Duchess of Portsmouth, Louise de Queraille:

Your noble pity and compassion found me, where I was far cast backward from my blessing, down in the rear of Fortune; call'd me up, plac'd me in the shine, and I have felt its comfort. You have in that restor'd me to my native Right, for a steady Faith, and Loyalty to my Prince, was all the Inheritance my Father left me. . . .

The ensuing praise of her young son, the Duke of Richmond, could possibly be construed as a polite indication of availability to serve as the boy's tutor, as he had instructed Nell Gwyn's son by the king. But beneath the superficial praise, there are some subtleties and peculiar ironies in Otway's choice of the duchess. "Madame Carwell," as she was called by the English, was at this time in collusion with Shaftesbury, for her own interests included promoting her son's possible claim to the throne. She was also corresponding with Louis XIV concerning the exclusion situation, and finding French financial support for the Whigs.

The Epilogue to *Venice Preserv'd* is full of unwitting ironies as well. Otway bravely asserts that "Poets in honour of the Truth shou'd write, / With the same Spirit brave men for it fight," and then goes on to declare that he is unafraid of a "Rose-Alley Cudgel Ambuscade." This alludes to Lord Rochester, who was so angered by his caricature in the *Essay on Satyr* that he allegedly hired some ruffians to deliver a beating to John Dryden in Rose Alley. Mulgrave, not Dryden, was the true author of the offending work, but it was believed that Louise de Queraille assisted Rochester in arranging the assault.[26] Furthermore, the concluding hymn of loyal praise to James cannot have pleased the royal mistress very well, involved as she was in his exclusion from succession. As far as flattering the Duchess is concerned, it seems that Otway could not possibly have blundered more if he had tried.

It might be presumptuous, but not wholly unreasonable, to argue that Otway knew perfectly well what he was doing in this dedication. He writes, "Forgive me then, Madam, if (as a poor Peasant once made a Present of an Apple to an Emperour) I bring this small Tribute . . . and lay it at your feet." The humility, even servility, of this sentence contrasts sharply with the significance of the allusion of the apple. Massinger's play *Emperor of the East* is the dramatization of an anecdote concerning the emperor Theodosius. Given a beautiful apple by a humble peasant, the Emperor gives it to his wife, Eudocia. She gives it to her lover who in turn, hoping to win favor in court, gives it to the Emperor again. Eudocia then lies when the suspicious Theodosius questions her and claims that she ate the apple. Theodosius banishes the lover and repudiates Eudocia. Otway, using this allusion, might be proffering a genuine apple of discord, while assuming that the simile will slip by unnoticed. It is in any case a piquant testimony to the troubled times that Otway might address ostensibly loyal praise to a lady who herself was a part of the conspiracy, a royal mistress who, like the character Aquilina in the play, had been trifling with both sides of a dangerous contest for power.

The portrait of Shaftesbury in the play is divided between the old rebel Renault and the old Senator Antonio, as Aline Mackenzie Taylor points out in her *Next to Shakespeare*.[27] Antonio is a senile, diseased old man, a sexual masochist who has stolen Pierre's mistress, the courtesan Aquilina whom he calls "Nicky-Nacky." Renault is a ferocious plotter whose zeal for revolution is accompanied by a frightening contempt for individuals: he tries to rape Belvidera, Jaffeir's wife, when she is placed in his care as a token of Jaffeir's loyalty to the cause. These two lecherous old men serve to illustrate Otway's point that both sides of the civil struggle have men who are vicious and corrupt.

Taylor argues that the dramatic energy of *Venice Preserv'd* is to be found in the personal motivation of the rebels Jaffeir and Pierre. Pierre, she says, has joined the cause out of resentment that Antonio stole his mistress. Jaffeir joins the plot because he resents his father-in-law, only to betray the cause, again out of resentment, when he learns of Renault's attack on his wife.[28] Because both Antonio and Renault are pernicious characters, Taylor believes that the audience's interest is focused primarily upon the personal feelings of the main figure. "All sympathy becomes divorced from the political opponents and rests with the three principals, in their misfortunes representative of the respectable, peaceable part of the nation, who are caught in the circumstances produced by a gigantic fraud and forced into courses of action that they would never have taken if left to their own devices."[29] But the question whether the central characters are forced into their decisions by circumstances or choice must be discussed later during an evaluation of the plays: here we are considering the effect of the political background of the play.

There can be no doubt that Otway views the times with horror, seeing everywhere the "busie heads" and "bloudy stratagems." Plots abounded. Not only was the king involved in secret pacts with Louis, but James's secretary, Coleman, had been found out in his correspondence with the French king's confessor to be discussing the conversion of English Protestants. The dubious Meal Tub Plot, a Catholic conspiracy concocted in the spirit of retaliation against the Popish Plot, had also been discovered.[30] On the Whig side were the unscrupulous allegations of Titus Oates and his fellow perjurers, and the political maneuvers of Shaftesbury and the Green Ribbon Club to force their Exclusion bills through Parliament.

In 1682 two very real plots were being worked out by the Whigs, one to organize a general insurrection and the other, later to be known as the Rye House Plot, to assassinate Charles and James.[31] It is therefore naive to think that the Restoration audience of *Venice Preserv'd* would fail to take seriously the political background of the play simply on the grounds that characters on both sides were vicious and cancelled each other out. Whig philosophers were arguing that there must be a separation of the king's natural person and his political person. This distinction alluded to in *The Poet's Complaint* "betwixt persons Naturall and Politick" must have deeply affected nearly everyone in public life at the time, just as we can see how it affected Madame Carwell. The question is how, under such circumstances, one may behave honorably and make the proper moral choices. Just because one takes sides with neither conspirators nor senate, for example, the political backdrop does not fade into insignificance. Rather it must have represented an intensification of reality to the Restoration audience, for none knew better than they that neutrality could be as compromising as partisanship.

The Venetian Senate is corrupt, mercilessly exploiting and victimizing the citizens. As Pierre says,

> We have neither Safety, Unity, nor Peace,
> For the foundation's lost of Common Good;
> Justice is lame as well as blind amongst us;
> The Laws (corrupted to their ends that make
>   'em)
> Serve but for Instruments of some new Tyranny,
> That every day starts up to enslave us deeper.

Priuli, a senator, has demonstrated the abuses the Senate is capable of by signing a commission permitting Jaffeir's estate to be put up for auction: his motivation is personal, for he hates Jaffeir for marrying his daughter Belvidera without his consent, but his revenge is public. The rebels recognize the deep division in Venice and it is their aim to exploit the weaknesses of the government and to purge the Senate by insurrection and assassination. Renault, the fiercest of them, explains:

> The Publick Stock's a Beggar, one Venetian
> Trusts not another: Look into their Stores
> Of general safety; Empty Magazines,
> A tatter'd Fleet, a murmuring unpaid Army,
> Bankrupt Nobility, a harrast Commonalty,
> A factious, giddy, and divided Senate,
> Is all the strength of Venice: Let's
> destroy it.

The rebels are as greedy and tyrannical as the senators they plot against. Jaffeir discovers this shortage of honor among them after offering his wife as a pledge of his dedication to the cause, only to find that she was attacked by Renault.

Nearly every succeeding generation of critics found the "Nicky-Nacky" scenes between Antonio and Aquilina to be a shocking lapse of taste. Bonamy Dobree cannot forgive Otway for them, reasoning that even if the poet "included the farcical lines at the King's request, he did not feel that they were amiss as part of his structure."[32] Let us then examine a portion of the play that was considered acceptable, Belvidera's account of Renault's attack:

> No sooner wert thou gone, and I alone,
> Left in the pow'r of that old Son of
> Mischief;
> No sooner was I lain on my sad Bed,
> But that vile Wretch approacht me; loose,
> unbutton'd,
> Ready for Violation . . .

Renault's attempt at rape may be considered tolerable because he is, after all, a wicked rebel and not a senator, because we only hear about it and do not see it, and because rape is not thought to be perverted, while flagellation is. We see Antonio begging to be whipped, and his masochism is presumably all the more distasteful because he is a senator.

Yet we have no right to assume with Dobree that Otway did not consider what he was doing by displaying sexual aberration on both sides of the political issue. It would make far more sense to consider that the Nicky-Nacky scenes are evidence of his general indictment of the Venetians, "A People nurst up equally with Vices / And loathsome Lusts, which Nature most abhors." To excise these scenes as later generations did is to remove the odor of decay from the Senate, leaving us only with Priuli's senile repudiation of his son-in-law to provide the sense of moral disintegration.

Renault, on the other side of the issue, never speaks conversationally. Every word he utters is a defiant exhortation to rebellion, and his is the most bloodthirsty of imagery:

> Without the least remorse then let's
> resolve
> With Fire and Sword t'exterminate these
> Tyrants;
> And when we shall behold those curst
> Tribunals,
> Stain'd by the Tears and sufferings of the
> Innocent,
> Burning with flames rather from Heav'n than
> ours,
> The raging furious and unpitying Souldier
> Pulling his reeking Dagger from the bosoms
> Of gasping Wretches; Death in every Quarter,
> With all that sad disorder can produce,
> To make a Spectacle of horror . . .

He is single-minded and calculating: he evaluates everything in terms of its relationship to the success of his plot. Renault is the deadly serious portrait of Shaftesbury, while Antonio is mainly the object of a cynical wit.

The political insight in *Venice Preserv'd* is almost unbelievably prophetic. The play was brought forth in 1682, not long after the

Whigs had scurried from Oxford, at a time when they were trying to rally and recover from the blow by selling tickets for a feast in London, intended to serve as a counterdemonstration to a feast planned the same night in honor of James. Charles forbade the celebration officially, as he had had to forbid the bonfires "honoring" his restoration to the throne, and the Tory poets were delighted. In his prologue to Aphra Behn's *The City Heiress,* Otway mocks the Whigs:

> Sham-Plots you may have paid for o'er and
> o'er;
> But who e'er paid for a Sham-Treat before?

The king, it was felt, was showing his true political strength at last, outwitting the Whigs at every turn and making fools of them to boot. Some Tories were prematurely satisfied that the political dissension was at last under control. Although *Venice Preserv'd* may have ridden the tide of this sense of victory, the play is, like *Caius Marius,* a sharp warning against complacency.

In the year following its first production, some of the dangers pointed by *Venice Preserv'd* came true. The Whigs had outlined, with Shaftesbury's knowledge, a plot to kill the royal brothers as they traveled from London to Newmarket. An accident prevented their making the journey, and thus was Rumbold's Rye House Plot discovered, bringing out great numbers of Jaffeirs hastening to betray the plan in return for clemency.[33] The chief plotter, Ferguson, for example testified that he had really been a double agent, staying in the plot because Monmouth had asked him to: he swore that at the last minute he and Rumbold would have intervened to save the king's life.

A general insurrection plot was also well underway in the winter of 1682–83, scheduled to begin in the spring. Shaftesbury's death in Holland in January may have caused the plan to lose some of its force, but its revelation brought still more conspirators into the open. Lord Howard was caught literally hiding behind his chimney and was dragged out to testify: upon his evidence, Russell and Sidney were convicted and executed for plotting insurrection. When Essex learned of this, he cut his throat in the Tower of London.[34] Sidney and Russell died with proud defiance, as did Pierre and Renault, preferring death to making a public declaration that subjects may not resist their sovereign:

Duke: Say; will you make confession
           Of your vile deeds and trust the
           Senate's mercy?

Pierre: Curst be your Senate: Curst your Constitution:
           The Curse of growing factions and division
           Still vex your Councils, shake your publick safety,
           And make the Robes of Government you wear,
           Hatefull to you, as these base Chains to me.

Duke: Pardon or death?

Pierre: Death, honorable death.

Renault: Death's the best thing we ask or you can give.

From the Whig standpoint, the way in which Sidney and Russell faced execution, refusing to recant, is the essence of the nobility of that long struggle against repression. Trevelyan speaks for the Whig historian when he writes, "Thus, these two men, on whom all eyes were turned in the days of the blackest ruin and shame that ever befell the cause of freedom in England, showed to the world in spite of the guilt and violence with which they themselves had helped to associate that cause, that liberty is a religion for which men who most enjoy life and love and power, can cheerfully lay down all these, because without liberty they are nothing." In this same fashion Otway damns the Venetian plot and yet ennobles the honorable men who preferred death to capitulation. In the epilogue he writes, with eerie foreshadowing:

> The Text is done, and now for Application,
> And when that's ended pass your Approbation.
> Though the Conspiracy's prevented here,
> Methinks I see another hatching there.

The political ambivalence in *Venice Preserv'd* contributes to its strength rather than its weakness. Addison, living in more stable times, objected: "This poet has founded his tragedy of *Venice Preserv'd* on so wrong a plot, that the greatest characters in it are those of rebels and traitors."[35] But this is the heart of the issue. Otway makes us see that, though the insurrection plot was wrong, honorable men like Jaffeir and Pierre participated in it for reasons of honor. When we reflect upon the reprehensible manner in which Charles signed death warrants against men whom he personally knew to be innocent victims of false testimony, the confusion of the times becomes apparent. The families and friends of these victims of Libell might easily feel bound to defend their honor and turn to the organized Whig opposition, just as Jaffeir and Pierre had done. Because the Restoration theater appealed to the aristocracy is not a reason to assume that it existed in a vacuum. The repercussions of the Exclusion Crisis shook the entire foundation of English society, and the drama was not excepted. Otway in particular had thought his way through to a new vision of the rather worn love-and-honor dilemma. The existential quality of the tragedy was immediately recognized as a profound new interpretation of honor and loyalty, and Otway's greatness was assured because *Venice Preserv'd* struck a nerve.

Chapter Three

The First Plays (1675—1678)

The Heroic Convention

While Restoration comedy has been rather widely and even enthusiastically read for its witty and "indecent" passages, the tragedies and heroic plays of the same era have been virtually ignored. *Venice Preserv'd* and Dryden's *All for Love, The Conquest of Granada,* and *Aureng-Zebe* are among the few relics of these forms still commonly anthologized to satisfy the curiosity of the student of literature. Not many people have read *Cleomenes, the Spartan Hero, Caius Marius, Sophonisba or Hannibal's Overthrow, Tyrannick Love,* or *Lucius Junius Brutus,* to name only a few of the plays written by only a few of the most popular playwrights, Otway, Lee and Dryden.

Since *The Rehearsal,* the Restoration tragic hero has been the object of merriment and scorn. As John Cunningham says of Almanzor, the central figure of Dryden's *Conquest of Granada,* "This is our typical Restoration hero, brave, boastful, and bone-headed, responding to certain stimuli like Pavlov's dogs slobbering."[1] After a brief discussion of the heroic Greek legends which served to provide the pattern and source for this kind of character, Cunningham notes, "The plumed and armoured Restoration actor, strutting on his green baize carpet, began with Achilles and Ajax, Hercules and Theseus; he ends in a comic strip—Garth and Superman."[2] Otway's biographer, Roswell Gray Ham, would not quarrel with this:

By contemporary usage these heroes of ranting tragedy were as variable as the moon, their changes dictated only by their boundless egoism.[3]

Clifford Leech believes that the extravagance of language, action, and scenery of the heroic plays must serve as a kind of escape from painful reality:

Thus the strained, operatic manner was suited to this presentation of distressed nobility, because the conception of nobility itself was remote from more ordinary hopes and fears and common conditions. Moreover, the heroic manner was valued for its own sake rather than for any end it might achieve.[4]

It is fair to generalize from comments such as these that the Restoration hero, for all his high-flown speech and neo-Platonic dogma (perhaps because of them), went out of style rather quickly and never returned. Despite the change in taste, however, we must remember that he ruled supreme for a time, during which playwrights and actors competed furiously to offer their audiences the most perfect, exalted and eloquent model of self-sufficient honor ever seen on the stage. That "perfection" of character should be susceptible to the vicissitudes of time, fashion, and language perhaps more rapidly than imperfection is not reason to assume that the ideals represented in heroic plays lacked validity for their audience.

A good deal of the critical attention given to heroic drama of this period tends to concentrate upon its links with the past or with the contemporary French classical drama, pointing out that because the theaters had been closed in England for so long under the Puritan Interregnum, Restoration playwrights were obliged either to pick up the literary threads of the first part of the century or to imitate what they knew of continental drama. This is an interesting scholarly effort, even a worthy one, but it fails to explain why heroic drama should be so popular with Restoration audiences, who were neither critics nor literary historians for the most part.

Leech has attempted to find a basis for that popularity in remarking the escapist appeal of these plays: still, escapist literature is seldom so "pure" that it does not portray implicitly relevant values and judgments. Elaborate historical and mythological settings in fact may, by virtue of their apparent remoteness, reach the sympathy of a wider audience than an explicitly contemporary topical drama. The stringency of the Licensing Act also precluded any possibility of direct allusion to contemporary politics. Though everyone will agree that Shakespeare's plays are permeated with Elizabethan political thought, few modern critics any more than their eighteenth- or nineteenth-century forbears seem interested that much Restoration tragedy dealt as well with important questions of the time.

It is no accident that civil war should be the setting of so many of these plays, for England had not only survived the Interregnum, but remained poised on the brink of civil turmoil for many years after the Restoration. Scheming courtesans, villainous generals, and treacherous ministers are stock figures in these stories, as are bedeviled monarchs, sly priests, and crazed mobs. Just as our own popular escapist literature, science fiction, derives energy and substance from many of our immediate political fears, the heroic plays appealed in disguise to comparable issues of the Exclusion Crisis era. They explored such problems as the uncurbed malice of a cruel dictator, the horrors of mob rule, "kangaroo" courts, the impact of traitors and perjurers upon a weak legal system and a strained government, and the question of the extent to which the king's "natural" person might impinge upon his official political decisions. It is important to observe that the heroes of these plays are rarely kings themselves, though they may be heirs-apparent: the *Mirror for Magistrates* advice to the ruler has been transformed to advising the successor. They serve kings, may be unjustly punished by kings and sometimes even conspire against them, but in general, like Superman, their first loyalty must be to their own transcendent vision of honor.

Since Otway's serious plays reflect the shifting values of the critical decade of 1675–1685, it might be worthwhile, before embarking on the analysis of his first play, to summarize the overall changes to be found in his work. His first two tragedies are written carefully within the established heroic mode, even to the point of rhyming couplets. Both plays deal with internal court difficulties faced by an unsteady monarch. In *Caius Marius,* however, Otway brings a partisan conflict in ancient Rome to the stage, complete with violently unpredictable mobs: the personal side of the plot is cribbed shamelessly from Shakespeare's *Romeo and Juliet.* This play reflects the sharp transition in Otway's own philosophy, and shows his confidence as a dramatist in stepping outside the traditional boundaries of the established genre as far as the political plot is concerned. *The Orphan* is domestic tragedy in the great tradition of *Othello,* dealing with the problem of free will versus original sin, the viper within. All this prepares the way for the circumstantial morality of *Venice Preserv'd,* which is unlike any other play of its time in this respect. Because an inclination toward sentimental drama and *tragedie larmoyante* was beginning to emerge, Otway's later plays were applauded for their depth of feeling and perfect expression of sentiment, but not for their philosophical or moral vision, which was presumed to be unacceptable by any but Restoration standards.

Otway was from the first intrigued with moral ambiguity and paradox. His characters find themselves in situations which suddenly expose their own deep ambivalence, so that they must confront themselves as well as the problem. In coming to terms with themselves, they may not behave gloriously in the eyes of the world, but their struggle for authenticity is deeply moving. Critics have never been able to reconcile their own contrary responses to Otway. Typically, like Hazlitt, they are deeply stirred by his work, yet they are vaguely conscious that his moral philosophy is somehow threatening to them and to the established definition of tragedy. Thus often, facing this paradox in themselves, critics have tried to praise the emotional texture of the plays while damning their lack of moral virtue, as is the case in this early nineteenth century critique from a biographical encyclopedia:

Venice Preserv'd, without a virtuous character except the heroine, never fails to excite the deepest interest. It is remarkable, that although its purpose was to paint the horrors and vices of popular insurrection, he has put into the mouth of his revolutionary hero such forcible declamation against corruptions of government, and such glowing sentiments of patriotism, that the representation has been thought unsafe in times of public discontent. This tragedy is contaminated with some scenes of gross and licentious buffoonery, that characterize the times as well as the man. There is no writer whom one would more wish to have lived in a better age, and with more moral and literary advantages, than Otway.[5]

Over and over, puzzled critics have expressed this wish that Otway might have lived longer, making one suspect that they long for more samples of his mature thought which might help them spell out more clearly the answer to their own conflicts.

Alcibiades

Alcibiades, Otway's first play, printed in 1675, shows the poet's effort to mold a hero in the popular pattern. Blessed with an invincible naivete and denied by the structure of the play any opportunity to demonstrate his capabilities as a man of decisive action, Alcibiades and Otway seem to wander somewhat baffled through this maiden effort, preoccupied chiefly by the hero's sweetly ingenuous love for his bride Timandra. He has had, we are told, an unusual career. He had been recently overthrown as the general of Athens by his rival Theramnes, so he fled promptly to Sparta, where, for reasons best known to the king of Sparta, he was immediately appointed a Spartan general. He has been compared in this behavior to Dryden's famous Almanzor, in *The Conquest of Granada,* who rose above conventional loyalties by fighting for the underdog no matter whose side was right. But Alcibiades for the most part chooses to keep his moral convictions on this matter to himself, imparting to us instead his Platonic opinions on perfect love.

In the prologue to this play Otway writes modestly of himself, "Thus though this Trifler never wrote before, / Yet Faith he ventur'd on the common score." Truly, there are no flashes of dramatic genius or poetic language to illuminate this play, but there is plenty of physical action leading up to the last act when corpses rapidly accumulate on stage. There is some rather incongruous visual display, notably a slightly baroque wedding masque involving pretty priestesses, roses, apples and spears, dance and song celebrating the vows of Alcibiades and Timandra. It is a typical heroic drama of the 1670s, but its lack of intellectual brilliance did not impede its acceptance. John Dryden, an aficionado of the heroic genre, wrote equally uninspired heroic plays—*Amboyna,* for example, and *Cleomenes, the Spartan Hero*—but like Grade B films, there was always an audience for them and so they continued to appear.

Alcibiades believes that his purity of heart will protect him in all circumstances, through all adversity:

> No, I've a guard of innocence too strong.
> Whilst I unspotted that and friendship bear,
> No danger is so great that I need fear.

Despite his experience as an Athenian general, this innocent turncoat has no comprehension of treachery. He cannot understand, for example, why he should be pursued by "the base passions of a lustful Queen." Her increasingly frenzied efforts to seduce him result only in his rather lame offer to love her as a sister. Otway himself was amused by the stubborn continence of his hero and later remarked that the historical Alcibiades would surely have had no such scruples:

For my Hero to do him right, was none of that squeamish Gentleman I make him, but would as little have boggl'd at the obliging the passion of a young and beautiful lady, as I should my self, had I the same opportunities, which I have given him.[6]

But frustrated passion destroys the queen's sanity utterly. Her rage drives her to the point of poisoning Alcibiades' wife, Timandra, and then stabbing the king to death, in the demented hope that by freeing him from marital obligations while simultaneously making it possible to offer him not only herself but the crown of Sparta, Alcibiades will at last find her charms irresistible.

Despite faulty characterization, the plot maintains a fair speed. Alcibiades, fresh from Athens, becomes an instant favorite of the king of Sparta, as well as the apple of the queen's lustful eye. His stardom inspires such jealousy in the king's chief adviser, Tissaphernes, that he begins plotting to dispatch Alcibiades as quickly as possible by poisoning the wine in his wedding-bowl. The attempt is thwarted when the king, to show his gratitude for Tissaphernes' loyalty, ceremoniously proffers the poisoned bowl first to him. He pretends to swoon so that he may spill the wine, but explanations become unnecessary for at that moment news arrives of an Athenian attack. Like Othello, Alcibiades must depart for battle on his wedding-night.

Between this act and the next a great deal happens. Alcibiades covers himself with glory by conquering and taking captive his former Athenian rival Theramnes. In addition, Patroclus, Tissaphernes' son, has saved his life and become his dearest friend. Tissaphernes tries unsuccessfully to persuade Patroclus that his hero is a traitor, but when this doesn't work, he goes to Theramnes' prison tent and offers to release him from his chains and assist him in raping Timandra in an ultimate act of revenge. Even the villainous Theramnes is awed by the audacity of this offer, and comments:

> No 'tis in age alone great Spirits are young:
> The Soul's but infant when the Body's strong.
> These hoary heads like grisly Comets are,
> Which always threaten ruin, death and war.

In the meantime the queen has failed in her first attempt at seduction, and so when Alcibiades, returning to his tent, finds Theramnes preparing to drag Timandra into the bushes, he runs him through with his sword. After twenty-one lines of incongruously begging Timandra's forgiveness, the Athenian dies. Even more incongruously, she forgives him. Patroclus has discovered his father in the above-mentioned bushes and knows now that he is the true traitor, a fact that makes the loyal son miserable.

Tissaphernes and the queen now join forces. She kills her husband, summons the guards and hysterically accuses Tissaphernes of the murder. He tries to stab her in the struggle, but fails, so she proceeds to Timandra's tent and poisons her. Timandra accepts the poison with unrealistic fatalism as the alternative to giving up Alcibiades, and then dies rather slowly during the next hundred lines of dialogue, allowing time for Alcibiades to return to the scene and learn what has happened. He turns briefly on the murderous queen, but then has second thoughts about killing her because she is "so base a thing" that her slaughter would "brand my Trophyes with eternal infamy." So he just calls her a "damn'd fiend" instead and plunges the dagger into his own heart. Defeated beyond hope, the queen stabs herself and collapses upon the accumulated heap of bodies. Within seconds Patroclus becomes king, and he promptly assumes the deceased king's habit of meditating aloud upon the perils of kingship:

> For how uneasily on Thrones they sit,
> That must like me be wretched to be great.

Alcibiades' sustaining philosophy through all this brouhaha is a kind of warmed-over Platonism which relieves him of the fear of death but otherwise adds little to his character. The recurrence of allusions to the loves of the soul, the Platonic consolation of unhappy lovers, is truly in "the common score" of heroic drama. The typical Restoration interpretation involves an insatiable craving for a postmortem union of lovers' souls, which can be an effective passion when lovers are parted or otherwise forbidden—by marriage to others, incest, or other taboo—an unearthly association. Timandra reveals an almost morbid preoccupation with death from the very first act of the play, however. As soon as Alcibiades leaves for war, she begins to reflect:

> But Death alone's th'unhappy Lovers ease,
> That seals up to us an Eternal Peace;
> By that our souls to endless pleasures move,
> And we enjoy an Everlasting Love.

When the Spartan queen at the last offers her the choice of forsaking Alcibiades or drinking poison, Timandra's philosophy points her way:

> Death is a blessing, and a thing so far
> Above that worst of all our frailties fear;
> It claims our joy, since by it we put on
> The top of happiness, perfection.

Eagerness to die for love is conventional in heroic drama. It can be quite moving in a totally hopeless situation, but obviously becomes rather silly when the problem can be set right.

The convention finds another application when Alcibiades offers to love the queen as a sister. Her contempt for this idea provokes him to try neo-Platonism as a strategem to calm her down. He says he must live true to Timandra, but he would die for the queen and then perhaps in the afterlife their souls could commingle: "With new imp't Zeal beyond the Stars wee'l fly, / There meet, and mingle to a Deity." The practical mistake of the stratagem is that the queen takes him seriously, but more important as far as the play is concerned, Alcibiades seems to misuse his spiritual convictions. Otway obviously does not have the language of souls in perfect command.

Personal motives of jealousy and lust prevail in bringing about this tragedy. Alcibiades' rather empty personality, however, makes the whole disaster take on the quality of a very nasty accident. Simply by his being handsome, dutiful, faithful, and in the wrong place at the wrong time, calamity overtakes him. It is Alcibiades' character, or lack of it, which flaws the play. The only genuine decision we see him make is his refusal to kill the queen. At this point his reasoning that she is "too Base" to die at his hands seems unconvincing, since he has never established himself as a person with a refined sense of honor. One suspects that Otway was uncertain of the propriety of having his hero kill a woman. "Besides I now must die," he comments rather offhandedly as he rejects the queen's final proposition. It is his duty to die when Timandra dies, and he accepts this responsibility almost with indifference, just as he shrugged his shoulders and set off to defend his new country on his wedding-night. He expresses no special human emotion, just perfunctory grief at the departing this life and an understandable vexation with the pestiferous queen. Alcibiades is truly what John Cunningham calls a "bone-headed" hero.

Politically this play is as innocent as its hero. Much maligned by the lustful and the corrupt, Alcibiades' decision to kill himself is based solely upon his longing to join his wife. The king, always so proud and confident of his court, is misled by his chief advisor and murdered by his sex-crazed wife. The Athenian general wants revenge on Alcibiades not so much for betraying his country as for marrying Timandra. Our hero is more baffled than tormented by all the strange conspiracies, but obtuse as he is about life, he thinks only in terms of being a loyal subject and a faithful husband. Therefore, with little more than a sigh of resignation, he dispatches his soul to eternity.

Otway resurrects the lustful Spartan queen, played by Mrs. Mary Lee, to recite his comic epilogue. Expressing her irritation that the poet was "forc't to make me rise for th'Epilogue," she denounces him to the audience:

> The fop damn'd me, but e're to hell I go,
> I'd very fain be satisfy'd, if you
> Think it not just that he were serv'd so too.

With these wry lines, which might indicate Otway's own dissatisfaction with the weaknesses of his neo-Platonic resolution, his maiden effort is launched: "Then damn him down to Hell, and never spare, / Perhaps he'l find more favour there than here."

Don Carlos

In his second play, *Don Carlos, Prince of Spain,* Otway forgives those who criticized his first effort and somewhat more confidently points out that some men "of good Judgement" believe that his new work "is the best Heroick Play that has been written of late."[7] Yet he has once again written a story primarily of love and jealousy in which personal intrigue predominates: an uxorious king, driven by jealousy bred of false counsel, kills his wife and his son. The plot is utterly conventional, the villains are reminiscent of those in *Alcibiades,* and the lovers are steeped in Platonic contemplation of their souls, but the poetic language has become more controlled and more involved with the thought and feelings of the characters. A new self-confidence appears in Otway's *Preface to the Reader.* "This I may modestly boast of . . . that it never fail'd to draw Tears from the Eyes of the Auditors, I mean those whose Souls were capable of so Noble a Pleasure."[8] The scene he is alluding to is what Eric Rothstein has described as a "long, lachrymose death scene after having ended an almost equally lachrymose life with suicide."[9] When we recall the feeling of numb indifference surrounding Alcibiades' expiration, also by suicide, we may appreciate why Otway was relieved to discover that he could provoke tears.

The play was a success. John Downes, the prompter, noted that it "lasted successively 10 days; it got more Money than any preceding Modern Tragedy."[10] Money and duration may be the main proofs of popular success, but there is other evidence as well. Otway reminds us proudly that both the king and the Duke of York had expressed "their good liking of it, and Encouragement to proceed."[11] Beyond praise, attention from fellow writers is another sign of success. In his preface, Otway cites a "fine Facetious witty Person" who apparently declared, "Igad he knew not a line in it he would be Author of." Dryden was fond of punctuating his speech with "y gads," as his lambasting in *The Rehearsal* emphasizes, so Otway here is most likely alluding to the laureate himself.

The lampoon which most aggrieved Otway appeared after the publication of *Don Carlos,* in the infamous *Tryal of the Poets for the Bays:*

> Tom Otway came next, Tom Shadwell's dear Zany,
> And swears for Heroicks, he writes best of any:

> Don Carlos his Pockets so amply had fill'd,
> That his Mange was quite cur'd, and his Lice
> were all Kill'd. [12]

Otway believed that Shadwell was responsible for this passage, when in fact it was almost certainly written by his aristocratic patron Lord Rochester.

Don Carlos, Prince of Spain is standard heroic fare, a story of love and court conspiracy entirely written in rhymed couplets. The character of the uxorious king who is driven to murder is comparable to that of the passionate queen in *Alcibiades* for the purpose it serves in precipitating the tragedy. But because Otway gives psychological depth and motivation to his character, this is no simple case of thwarted lust.

The king had chosen a beautiful young French bride for his son Don Carlos, but during their courtship he decided to marry her himself. On their wedding night, when the play begins, as the king takes his wife to bed he admonishes his son to "let thy Father's happiness be thine." This is painful advice for the young man, for he had fallen in love with the girl before his father had so peremptorily changed the plans. Don Carlos is a loyal son and subject, however, so he mopes and sulks like Achilles in his tent and tries lamely to resign himself to the situation.

The new queen is unhappy with the contract which made her "an offering to Philip's bed," but she interprets her marital duty as being the "Interest and Safety of the State," requiring unimpeachable fidelity to the king. Don Carlos cannot resist reminding her of his love, and she is powerfully moved. He assures her that his innocence is perfect and his wishes are pure, and he begs her to let him continue in this unsullied devotion. She grants him permission to love her in this fashion, reminding him:

> Yet keep the Flame so pure, such chast desire,
> That without spot hereafter we above
> May meet when we shall come all soul all love.

Here a rare stage direction reads, "Gives her hand, which D. Carlos during all this speech kisses eagerly." The painful Platonism of the moment is as appropriate here as it was inappropriate in *Alcibiades,* for the lovers are bound in honor to their obligation to the king, while the "Flame" of desire is betrayed by the urgent hand-kissing. The king, meanwhile, has had his Spanish jealousy aroused by his evil counselor Rui-Gomez and has already decided that, "If she prove false, as yet I fear, she dyes."

The characters Rui-Gomez and the Duchess of Eboli are comparable in function to Iago and Emilia of *Othello*. Gomez has been coveting the throne for all the years he has served as Don Carlos's guardian, while the Duchess has been studying the arts of love to serve her ambition of becoming queen of Spain by means of "practic'd Charms." The night of the royal wedding they discover each other, and form an alliance to undermine the monarchy. Rui-Gomez compares himself to a bee in the role he plans to play:

> . . . methinks I view from hence a King,
> A Queen and Prince, three goodly Flowers spring,
> Whilst on 'em like a subtle Bee I'l prey,
> Till so their Strength and Vertue drawn away,
> Unable to recover, each shall droop,
> Grow pale and fading hang his Wither'd Top:
> Then fraught with Thyme Triumphant back I'l
>   come
> And unlade all the pretious sweets at home.

The king is patterned after Othello in the intensity of his jealousy, yet Otway has added the interesting psychological dimension of a father's guilty envy of his son's youthful masculinity. The factor which makes him vulnerable to the Iago-like counsel of Rui-Gomez is not his love for the queen but rather the profound fear that he is not the man his son is. It is on this insecurity that the king unwittingly conspires in the design of his own ruin. Otway, more than any other Restoration poet, is aware of the vast and subtle power of sexuality, and the characterization of the king reflects this sensitivity.

In contrast with the repression embodied in the impossible triangle, Otway provides a new sort of character, a libertine philosopher, Don John of Austria. While the central characters struggle in their triple bind with desire and frustration and loyalty, Don John, the bastard son of the king of Austria, is given almost a choral voice introducing the second and third acts with his meditations in an orange grove. His theme is always freedom—the freedom to serve natural rather than human law—and his preoccupation seems founded upon the very condition of his illegitimacy:

> Why should dull Law rule Nature, who first made
> That law, by which her self is now betray'd?
> E're Man's Corruptions made him wretched, he
> Was born most noble that was born most free:
> Each of himself was Lord; and unconfin'd
> Obey'd the dictates of his Godlike mind.
> Law was an Innovation brought in since,
> When Fools began to love Obedience,
> And call'd their slavery Safety and Defence.

His radical opinions contrast sharply with the constrained situation developing in the court. Instead of shame at being a bastard, his philosophy affords him a measure of pride which in this speech approaches blasphemy:

> My Glorious Father got me in his heat,
> When all he did was eminently great . . .
> Why should it be a Stain upon my Blood
> Because I came not in the Common Road,
> But Born obscure and so more like a God?

Don John is a philosophizing libertine, a character more commonly found in comedy than in serious drama: such figures as Harry Horner in *The Country Wife* (1675) and Manly in *The Plain Dealer* (1676), both by William Wycherley. On a more confined scale, Dorimant in Etherege's *Man of Mode* (1676), cherishes his liberty and is contemptuous of social institutions. Freedom to follow nature is the wellspring of the libertine philosophy: conventional behavior, following as it does the artificial rules of society, is a form of slavery. In love, the libertine believes in emulating the sparrow, which is to follow his natural affections and eschew monogamy at all costs. In religion, he is an atheist, rejecting the institution of the church and its sacraments for imposing hypocritical restraints on behavior. In politics, he is "independent," because of the dishonesty and corruption he sees in the court. He believes in natural heroes over inherited titles, hence Don John's "born obscure and so more like a God." He is generally clear-sighted concerning his own purposes in life, and therefore he usually feels free to consider himself an enlightened Machiavel in attaining his objectives.

Don John, at the beginning of the play, is enjoying an uninhibited affair with the Duchess of Eboli. His meditation on love is consistent with his libertine principles:

> How vainly would dull Moralists Impose
> Limits on Love, whose Nature brooks no Laws:
> Love is a God, and like a God should be
> Inconstant: with unbounded liberty
> Rove as he list.---

In sharp contrast to the ethereal preoccupations of the Platonic lovers in the play, Don John aligns his desires with those of Jove:

> Alas lay this Religion now Aside;
> I'le show thee one more pleasant, that which
> Jove
> Set forth to the old World, when from above
> He came himself and taught his Mortals Love.

When the Duchess of Eboli proves deceitful, he abandons her and concentrates upon attempting to reconcile the king with Don Carlos. He is the most clear-headed character in the play: because of his perspective as a freeman, he can see through the distortions and the villanous hypocrisies in which the lovers and the courtiers have entangled themselves. He promises Don Carlos his loyalty and protection and he tries to reason with the king, all to no avail. The king insists that his son must be disinherited in favor of Don John. Don John declines the offer because it wrongs his nephew, and the king accuses him of naivete: "Thou living free, alas, art easie grown, / And think'st all hearts as honest as thy own." To which Don John replies:

> Not Sir so easie! as I must be bold,
> And speak what you perhaps wou'd have untold;
> That y'are a slave to th'vilest that obey,
> Such as Disgrace on Royal Favour lay:
> And blindly follow as they lead astray.
> Voracious Varlets, sordid Hangers on,
> Best by familiarity Th'are known,
> Yet shrink at frowns, but when you smile
> they fawn.

Despite his best efforts, the snares of passion and deceit work their inevitable catastrophe. The king arranges to have the queen poisoned, and arrests his son as a traitor. Don Carlos chooses a Senecan suicide and cuts his veins in the bathtub. Just as he and the young queen are close to death, they are brought together before the king who has too late discovered his mistake and now wishes to beg their forgiveness. Great souls that they are, they forgive him generously in their last breaths, and die. The king murders Rui-Gomez on the spot for his false counsel, and promptly goes mad.

Don John is the Fortinbras of the play: he assumes the responsibility of the throne, postpones love, and sets off for the foreign war that had been neglected all this time. Otway has improved upon his formula in *Alcibiades* by giving more depth and breadth to the role of the hero's confidant. It is a successful and effective device, and Otway reworks it later in *The Orphan* and in *Venice Preserv'd*. The pair of friends, one a lover and one a philosopher, became a kind of trademark of his, so that the spurious *Heroick Friendship* was centered on this device to persuade the gullible that it surely was Otway's lost manuscript.

The Double Bill: *Titus and Berenice* and *The Cheats of Scapin*

Only six months after the triumph of *Don Carlos,* Otway provided the Duke's Company with another success. The prompter Downes remarked upon the first performance of *Titus and Berenice* and *The Cheats of Scapin* their "being perfectly well *Acted*; had good Success."[13] Both plays are condensations of French classics by Racine and Molière respectively. The stylish Francophile audience must have relished the delightful evening of theater which Otway presented them with at the height of the Christmas holiday entertainments. His miniaturization of the French plays was both skillful and as faithful as possible under the circumstances to the spirit and language of the originals. The acting was excellent, featuring Betterton, Smith, and Mrs. Lee as the three tragic characters, and the incomparable team of Anthony Leigh and Robert Nokes as Scapin and Gripe. Such polish and professionalism was certain to be warmly received.

But a frosty reception awaited Otway in another quarter, for his double bill had stolen the thunder from two established playwrights, Crowne and Ravenscroft, who were working up their own full-length versions of the French plays. Crowne had been working on *The Destruction of Jerusalem* for months: it was to be a two-part tragedy, massive in its scope and extravagance, to be presented in two consecutive evenings. It was expanded, rather than miniaturized, and given what Dryden would label "English" breadth and vigor. This sweepingly imaginative adaptation transformed Racine's stark neoclassical drama into a bold heroic pageant of love and war. Crowne was under contract to submit all his work first to Betterton's company, and so he was legitimately angry when the Duke's Company refused the play for the reason that Otway's version was already in rehearsal. Although he hastened to bring *The Destruction of Jerusalem* to the competing theater where it was accepted, Crowne remained bitter toward Otway. In his "Epistle to the Reader" Crowne calls Otway a plagiarist:

Some persons accus'd me of stealing the parts of Titus and Berenice from the French play written by Mr. Racine on the same subject; but a Gentleman having lately translated that Play, and expos'd it to Publique view on the Stage, has sav'd me that labour, and vindicat'd me better than I can my self.[14]

Titus and Berenice, in three acts instead of five, reduces Racine's eloquence and psychological depth to the level of a scene of wistful parting. Of necessity, Otway eliminates nearly all of the "outside world" from his plot in order to dwell—briefly—upon the personal relationships of Titus, the ruler of Rome; Berenice, Queen of Jerusalem, who captured his love when he conquered her country; and Antiochus, King of Syria, who harbors a steadfast but hopeless passion for Berenice. We must accept, rather than see, that Titus' cruel nature, fostered in the court of Nero, has been utterly changed by the virtue of Berenice and the noble sweetness of love. The former tyrant is shown here only as a sad and gentle lover who is forbidden by Roman law to marry a foreign woman. As the play opens, Titus is trying to steel his heart against Berenice without success, hoping that his feigned indifference will turn her affections from him. Instead she becomes distracted and miserably unhappy by this sudden change in his attitude toward her. Antiochus reveals in the first scene his own adoration for Berenice, as well as his deep friendship and loyalty to Titus: in the second act he confesses these feelings directly to the lovers, and all three of them brood about the pitiful situation they find themselves in.

This is Otway's last play written in rhymed couplets. The discomfort of the trio of hopeless lovers can hardly compare with the stiffness of the meter and rhyme. Not even *Alcibiades* displays such arthritic verse. When Berenice is told at last that Titus loves her but cannot marry her, for example, she responds with these lines:

> From this sad Moment never more to meet,
> Is it for day to dawn, and day to set,
> In which I must not find my hopes still young,
> Nor yet once see my Titus all day long?
> Heav'ns how I wildly rave—to lose my pains
> On him ungrateful that my tears disdains!
> Of all those days of absence I shall count,
> With him, the number will to nothing mount.

In his fidelity to the original French, Otway betrays his own gift for rousing the passions. Nothing could be less spontaneous than this verse, but perhaps the audience tolerated it out of an awareness of its lofty aspirations—or more likely, confidence that the Molière piece was shortly to follow. At the end of the play, Titus puts Berenice and her kingdom in the care of Antiochus, who is by now suicidal. Berenice talks him out of self-destruction with these virtuous words:

> Let us all three a rare example prove:
> Of a most tender though unhappy love.

And Titus resolves to revert to his formerly vicious personality because he is condemned to live on without his angel:

> I'le try how much a Tyrant I can be.
> Henceforth all thoughts of pitty I'le disown,
> And with my arms the Universe ore-run;
> Rob'd of my Love, through ruins purchase fame,
> And make the world's as wretched as I am.

In his dedicatory epistle to Rochester, Otway is critical of the impertinence of contemporary audiences who believe themselves capable of discriminating judgment. To become one of these self-proclaimed wits, he says, merely requires "a very little French breeding, much assurance, with a great deal of talk and no sence."[15] If his contemptuous assessment is correct, it may offer an insight into their acceptance of *Titus and Berenice*.

The Cheats of Scapin, taken from Molière's *Les Fourberies de Scapin,* concluded and relieved the evening's entertainment with riotous farce. Ravenscroft, like Crowne, had been writing a full-length version of the French original at the time, and he too was put off by Otway's abbreviated adaptation:

> Very unfortunate this Play has bin;
> A slippery trick was play'd us by Scapin.
> Whilst here our Actors made a long delay,
> When some were idle, others run away,
> The City House comes out with half our Play.[16]

Ravenscroft had by this time adapted three of Molière's plays for the London stage. He was, according to John Wilcox, "the most facile and most shameless plagiarist of the period," possessing "an unusual knack for achieving theatrical success without solid merit."[17] Wilcox praises Otway's *Cheats of Scapin* as "the most creditable translation Molière had yet had."[18]

This farce maintains such a swift pace that there is little time to ponder the absurd contrivances of the plot. Scapin, the mischief-maker, keeps everyone in delightful turmoil, like a master juggler keeping hoops and dishes and balls spinning in wild defiance of gravity. The part requires a comedian who is capable of playing several different roles simultaneously, as we shall see. Molière wrote the part for himself, and Otway adapted it to the special talents of Anthony Leigh. In *An Apology for His Life,* Colley Cibber recalls Leigh as an actor "of the mercurial kind" who "in humour . . . loved to take a full career, but was careful enough to stop short, when just upon the precipice."[19] This is the beginning of a close association between playwright and comedian, for Leigh was to play the sly Malagene in *Friendship in Fashion,* Sir Jolly Jumble in *The Soldier's Fortune,* and the "Nicky-Nacky" impersonation of Shaftesbury in *Venice Preserv'd.* When this brilliant actor died, a number of plays died with him: "by seeing no more of Leigh . . . in them the characters were quite sunk and alter'd."[20]

Structurally, this is classical farce. Two fathers have arranged between themselves that their sons will marry each other's daughter. The headstrong sons have married for love against their fathers' wishes, one to the daughter of a shipwrecked widow, one to a gypsy girl: these exotic ladies are in fact the two daughters intended for them. The fathers are absurdly mercenary and conservative, and the children are both rebellious and terrified of their fathers' fury. Each side appeals for assistance to Scapin who, as the very embodiment of comic anarchy, cozens them all into behaving like greater idiots than they already are while amply lining his own pockets. His final "cheat" is to trick them all into forgiving him for his mischief.

Scapin is a master of double-talk. In consoling old Thrifty over his son's rash marriage, he is suddenly reminded of a proverb:

When the Master of a Family shall be absent any considerable time from his home or Mansion, he ought rationally, gravely, wisely, and Philosophically, to revolve within his mind all the concurrent Circumstances, that may during the Interval conspire to the Conjunction of those misfortunes, and troublesome accidents, that may intervene upon the said absence, and the interruption of his Oeconomical inspection, into the remissness, negligences, frailties, and huge and perillous Errours, which his Substitutes, Servants, or Trustees, may be capable of, or liable and obnoxious unto. . . .

To which the confounded Thrifty replies, "S'death! Is all this a Proverb?"

The scene for which *The Cheats of Scapin* is most famous shows the trickster duping Gripe, the other old father, into climbing into a large sack for protection from an imaginary band of ruffians. Scapin proceeds to create the entire attack, meanwhile beating the sack convincingly. Otway Anglicized the scene by mimicking Welsh, Lancashire and Irish dialect, as well as broken French. At the height of the silliness a stage direction requires Tony Leigh to "Act a number of e'm together:"

We mun go this way—o' th' right hand, no to th' left hand—*lye close*—search everywhere—by my salvation, I will kill the dam Dog—and we do catch en, we'll tear 'en in pieces, and I do heer he went thick way—no streight forward. Hold, here is his Man, where's your Master—Dam me, where? in Hell? speak—*hold, not so furiously*—and you don't tell us where he is, we'll murder thee.

But Gripe peeps out of the sack and discovers the trick, and Scapin takes to his heels. This is followed by the felicitous discovery that the sons have married the appropriate daughters by choice instead of design, and the fathers are so relieved that they call for a merry feast. The farce concludes with a traditional marriage revel, and even Scapin, pretending now to be grievously wounded and prodigiously bandaged, is welcomed to the festivities and forgiven.

Otway's *Scapin* is as light and charming as *Titus and Berenice* is leaden, and the acclaim it earned encouraged him to try his hand at an original comedy. In a number of ways, this double bill signals the end of the twenty-four-year-old playwright's apprenticeship in the theater and marks his acceptance as a thorough professional. He now has a sure sense of the audience's tastes for pathos and farce, and has whipped together a crowd-pleasing entertainment. Despite the lack of originality in these two little plays, their success warrants his being taken seriously. He has also earned the full-fledged wrath of two established playwrights, Crowne and Ravenscroft, which can be considered a puberty rite in itself.

Otway has learned some lessons in translation from these efforts as well. Fidelity to Racine's eloquent lines, for one, results in unnatural complications of English syntax, a sense of wrestling mightily with sentence structure for the sake of achieving rhyme. The high declamatory style of Restoration acting might uphold the solemn dignity of the story of *Titus and Berenice,* but only with a certain amount of strain. In *The Cheats of Scapin,* however, Otway has maintained the sense of the original as well as keeping faithful to the language. He has Anglicized the humor when necessary, to great effect.

The effort of condensation involves some useful lessons as well. Otway was obliged to eliminate large portions of the source plays while maintaining a clear dramatic focus. In this he was again more successful with the comedy than the tragedy, for reasons that are immediately apparent. The leisurely development of tragedy's psychological passions is impossible in a condensation, where there is no time to spare for rumination and self-analysis. But Molière's whirlwind farce does not suffer in the same ways: if anything, translation proves to be a higher education in comic plotting, focus, and above all, timing.

Otway is clearly writing to the capabilities of the actors in the Duke's Company for the first time, and their special virtuosities are distinctly related to the popular success of the double bill. Mrs. Barry and Tony Leigh will figure prominently in his next play, *Friendship in Fashion,* and their parts are clearly written for them. Leigh's physical drollery and skill at vocal mimicry are used here to the full, as is Mrs. Barry's capacity to soar rapidly into a towering rage.

Even the prologue and epilogue exude a new self-confidence. Appealing no longer to the patience, good will, or even pity of his audience, he (in keeping with the fashion of that year) rails at them for their bad manners in the theater, jumping on the stage or carrying on noisy seductions in the boxes. He accuses the ladies of quality, who have taken to wearing visors to disguise themselves, of being "poachers" who take trade away from professional prostitutes. His dedication to Lord Rochester, the model for fashionable libertinism, assumes the tone of one urbane wit addressing another: "Never was Poetry under so great an oppression as now, as full of Phanatacism's as Religion, where every one pretends to the Spirit of Wit, sets up a Doctrine of his own, and hates a Poet worse than a Quaker does a Priest." The twenty-four-year-old playwright addresses his thirty-year-old patron with an air of jaded sophistication which betrays his newfound confidence. He is at the peak he describes in *The Poet's Complaint of His Muse,* just before developing a case of writer's block:

> Nay, by my Muse too I was blest
> With Off-springs of the choicest kinds,
> Such as have pleas'd the noblest minds,
> And been approv'd by Judgements of the best.
> But in this most transporting height,
> Whence I lookt down, and laught at Fate,
> All of a sudden I was alter'd grown;
> I round me lookt, and found my self alone:
> My faithless Muse, my faithless Muse was gone.

Chapter Four

Otway's Peak Season (1678–1680)

Friendship in Fashion

The decade of the 1670s, which saw the death of Milton and the bold Whig challenges to the monarchy, also marked the emergence of a new sort of comedy. Etherege's *The Man of Mode* and Wycherley's *The Country Wife* and *The Plain Dealer,* which appeared in 1675–76, brought with them a new sharpness and acidity of social observation that developed the special quality of Restoration wit. The comedy of manners assumes a new posture of fathomless cynicism, challenging any set of beliefs or value system to a test of hypocrisy. The libertine-gallants who thus throw down the gauntlet fearlessly expose the craven self-delusions which they believe to be at the heart of all social behavior.

At the time of their production Otway's comedies were attacked for sexual indecency, aesthetic improprieties, allegedly libelous portraits of members of court, and general want of wit. Twentieth-century critics of Restoration comedies in general and of Otway's comedies in particular make virtually the same charges. Because his first original comedy, *Friendship in Fashion,* was criticized on all these fronts we may properly address ourselves to the nature of the "unlucky censures" which had been passed upon this play. The prologue carefully denies that there is any wit, libel, or bawdy to be found here, preparing us, of course, for all three.

> I'th' next place, Ladies, there's no Bawdy in't,
> No, not so much as one well-meaning hint:
> Nay more, 'twas written every word he says
> On strictest Vigils and on Fasting Days,
> When he his Flesh to Pennance did enjoin . . .

Since the play opens with a rousing discussion of whoring, provoked by the delivery of a *billet-doux* from an amorous anonymous lady, we cannot possibly mistake Otway's intentions. Goodvile, the married libertine (a contradiction in terms), boasts of his conquests and the debaucheries he resumed ten days after his wedding. He explains how he allows his wife her freedom so that he may maintain his. Though marriage is essentially tiresome, he notes that it has its moments:

Mine is such a fond wanton Ape, I never come home, but she entertains me with fresh kindness: and Jack when I have been hunting for Game with you, and miss'd of an Opportunity, stops a Gap well enough.

To which his bachelor friend Truman replies:

There's no Condition so wretched but has its reserve: your Spaniel turn'd out of doors goes contentedly to his Kennel. Your Beggar when he can get no better lodging, knows his old warm Bush; and your married Whore-master that misses of his Wench, goes honestly home, and there's Madam Wife.

This opening dialogue serves well enough to illustrate the sort of nonchalant and amoral posturing which characterize the Restoration gallant of the 1670s. We recognize in the epigrammatic style, the sustained series of analogies, the sexual double-entendres ("kennel," "old warm Bush," "Madam Wife"), and the world-weary ironies that these characters are merely pretending to be men of wit and urbanity. It is a mistake to confuse the masquerade of wit with true wit, for the action of the comedy necessarily exposes falsity and passes its own sort of justice. The philandering husband appropriately becomes a cuckold; the betrayed mistress has her revenge upon the seducer; the unwary, the greedy, and the gullible are paraded about by the nose, in order that folly and affectation may be stripped, exposed, and scourged. For all its superficially fashionable amorality, this play works closely within its own ethical code.

Friendship in Fashion deals almost exclusively with sexual opportunism, a subject which critics for three hundred years have found difficult to deal with. In his epilogue to the play, spoken by Mrs. Barry appropriately enough, Otway shows that he recognizes its difficulty:

The Marry'd Sparks I know this Play will curse
For the Wifes sake, but some of 'em have worse.

Much of the critical malaise which has been recorded upon the subject of this play has been provoked by the fact that the women here are in as open pursuit of sexual adventure as the men. Otway indicts sexual opportunism in both sexes impartially, but his refusal to portray a double standard seems to have been a kind of mortal sin.

The characters in *Friendship in Fashion* represent the very antithesis of friendship and only the thinnest veneer of fashion. The Goodviles, married a year, are weary of each other. To avoid an excess of monogamous companionship, apparently, they seem to maintain an endless house party for their equally idle friends, who come and go at their pleasure, sponging the hospitality and exchanging the malicious gossip of the truly bored. The Goodviles are rich country gentry who try to stay away from the fresh air as much as possible, returning to their estate in the hinterlands only to collect tithes and, in Goodvile's case, claim *le droit du seigneur* from the tenants' prettiest daughters.

Mr. Goodvile feels obliged to spend a great deal of time keeping the knowledge of his indiscretions from his wife. He compares Mrs. Goodvile to a garment worn too long and to a tight shoe: the idea of returning to her, he insists crudely, is unthinkable—"I will sooner return to my Vomit." He is desperately busy trying to find a husband for his cast-off mistress Victoria, whose physical and mental distress, combined with the urgency of his efforts, plainly suggests that she is pregnant. In addition to all this, he is in ardent pursuit of a young lady named Camilla, whom he plans elaborately to seduce that night in his garden.

Mrs. Goodvile in turn is interested in her own affairs. She plots to have some time alone with young Truman, who is amused to pay her court surreptitiously in the presence of her husband. Naturally she is not unaware of Goodvile's lecherous entanglements, and her second order of business is to catch her husband in his own traps and to make him pay dearly for his philandering.

Their other guests include Valentine, a young gallant who is properly interested in, and suited to, the lady Camilla. The aging coquette Lady Squeamish, a hypocritically prudish old bawd, is contriving the seduction of Valentine. Her nephew, Sir Noble Clumsey, accompanies her everywhere: he is a wealthy bumpkin who is trying to acquire some polish and finesse among these stylish "friends," but he has a notoriously weak head, particularly for drink. Lady Squeamish's fleet of fops, who follow her in full sail, include a mincing, lisping pair named Caper and Saunter, as well as a nasty meddling gossip, Goodvile's cousin Malagene.

With the aid of a perfect copy of Camilla's ball-gown and the flattering cover of evening shadows, Lady Squeamish plots to trick Valentine into making love to her. But it is Goodvile, not Valentine, who pursues the blue gown into the bushes, and the disgust evinced by both of them upon discovering their true partners is genuinely funny, for the two lechers have been set upon each other. At the same time that Goodvile and Squeamish are engaged in their "feast of delight," Mrs. Goodvile and Truman are across the stage back of another hedge. As Truman puts it, "He'll never dream in what posture his own affairs stand in another place." Offstage, Valentine is with the real Camilla and the cast-off Victoria is thoughtfully considering the drunken marriage proposal of Sir Noble Clumsey, who has removed his shirt and lost his periwig and is sitting on the floor with the musicians. Thus are all eight major characters variously and simultaneously engaged in "feasts of delight," refuting the claim that "there's no Bawdy in't, / No, not so much as one well-meaning hint."

As for "well-meaning hints," they are sometimes too blunt to be called *double-entendres*. "My Lady will have her humour; but she's a very good woman at the bottom," says Sir Noble Clumsey of his aunt. And when Lady Squeamish feigns mourning at the separation of Mrs. Goodvile from her husband, Malagene (who is one of Otway's notorious voyeurs and has been hiding in the garden to observe the various encounters) says to her pointedly, "Goodvile you say—hark you my Dear, were he here in person, I would first of all decently kick him out of doors, then turn up thy Keel and discover here to my kinswoman what a leaky Vessel thou art."

An impressive feature of *Friendship in Fashion* is Otway's ability to maintain so much farcical activity onstage without neglecting the individual motivation and temperament of his characters. The play is extremely well plotted, and there are virtually no unexplained coincidences. Though there are a great many characters bustling about, each is clearly identifiable and carefully supplied with motivation for his or her behavior. Even the two gallants, Truman and Valentine, and the two preposterous foplings, Caper and Saunter, are carefully drawn as discrete individuals when they might, in the hands of another Restoration playwright, have been virtually interchangeable.

Some of the characters are even quite sympathetic, considering the circumstances of the play. Victoria, for example, is a kind, clear-thinking woman who realizes that although she is definitely in a compromised position, she has a duty to respect herself and to prevent Mr. Goodvile from betraying others as ruthlessly as he did her. Sir Noble Clumsey, the bumpkin who cannot master fashionable manners and does not know how to drink, is more than one might expect of such a "type"; he is an honest young man "at the bottom" and his compassion and basic amiability balance out his ineptitude in his favor. Therefore in spite of the implied joke about Victoria's pregnancy in the final scene when Lady Squeamish announces their betrothal—"she has accepted the title of my Lady Clumsey"—we are pleased by the match and not contemptuous as we might have been were the characters more superficial. Such attention to minor characters makes the play memorable, and though there is a good deal more activity than there is clever conversation, all the madness on stage is thoughtfully contrived by the playwright in human terms. Its bawdiness is funny because the people are funny, and gross when the people are gross.

Goodvile's corruption is exposed by Victoria and Mrs. Goodvile, who collaborate to have their revenge on him. Though he most probably will never reform, we know at least that he cannot deceive his wife (nor she him) as they pursue their fashionable friendships in the future. Demanding that comedy "correct" immoral behavior in the sense of forcing a dramatic reformation upon a lecher like Goodvile, whose wife after all is also a sexual opportunist, is too much to ask. It is morally and aesthetically sufficient that he be confounded in his exploits at every turn, that he should make love to old Lady Squeamish instead of Camilla, that he become a well-known cuckold, and that his selfish designs lead him beyond exasperation by the end of the play. He is repaid in kind and quantity quite appropriately for his excesses.

In addition to its hectic activity, *Friendship in Fashion* contains a running theme of comment upon the Restoration theater. Lady Squeamish, whose character is borrowed from William Wycherley's *The Country Wife,* fancies herself abreast of all the latest literary opinions. In her critical prattle we recognize the sublimation of her elderly lust, for since her chief interest in life is sex, her chief literary preoccupations are sexual. Nobody is fooled when she protests that "their Comedies now a days are the filthiest things, full of Bawdy and

nauseous doings which they mistake for raillery and intrigue; besides
they have no wit in'em, neither." She loves the love in a tragedy because
it is so "moving": "I love a Tragedy that moves mightily," she sighs.

Sir Noble Clumsey makes an alcoholic confession that he is an
aspiring poet: "I have written three Acts of a Play, and have nam'd it
already. 'Tis to be a Tragedy." Lady Squeamish hastens to counsel him
on writing the love scenes:

> Oh Cousin, if you undertake to write a
> Tragedy, take my counsel: Be sure to say
> soft melting tender things in it that may
> be moving, and make your Ladies Characters
> vertuous what ere you do.

"Moving" tragedy with virtuous ladies was already a part of Otway's
reputation, and would eventually become a touchstone for his critics for
centuries, so it is both amusing to note his allusion to himself and
sobering to reflect that whatever the superficial Squeamish admires
must by definition be silly. Sir Noble's play, as it turns out, is "the
pretty'st Plot and so full of waggery." When asked for the title, he
recalls with some effort: "Why let me see; 'Tis to be call'd *The Merry
Conceits of Love; or the Life and Death of the Emperour Charles the Fifth, with
the humours of his Dog Bobadillo."* When his companions protest that this
sounds more like a comedy than a tragedy, Sir Noble insists that it is the
latter because the dog Bobadillo is to be killed during the play.

The sly voyeur Malagene, played by Anthony Leigh, is a self-
proclaimed actor. As in *The Cheats of Scapin,* Otway gives Leigh free rein
to improvise as he pleases, with directions like "Malagene acts" or
"Malagene speaks in Punchinello's voice." From the sketches of Harle-
quin and Punchinello, we know that Otway was familiar with the
commedia dell'arte, but in the following passage we are shown a glimpse
of the Restoration "method" actor:

> Mal. I can act Punchinello, Scaramouchio, Harlequin, Prince
>   Prettyman, or any thing. I can act the rumbling of a Wheel-
>   barrow. Nay, more than that, I can act a Sow and Piggs,
>   Sausages a broiling, a Shoulder of Mutton a roasting: I can act
>   a Fly in a Honey-Pot.
>
> Tru. That indeed must be the effect of very curious observation.

Mal.   No, hang it, I never make it my business to observe any thing, that is Mechanick.

We must inevitably assume that all this is punctuated by ingenious demonstrations of mimicry, specifically written for Tony Leigh.

No less than fifteen songs punctuate the festivities, and from the second act onward musicians are involved in the action, emerging whenever someone calls for the fiddles, and growing gradually as drunk as Sir Noble Clumsey. By the fifth act it is reported that Malagene and Sir Noble have stolen the key from the sleeping butler, "And there they are with the Fat-Red-Fac'd Fidler that plays upon the Base, sitting Cross-leg'd upon the Floor, stript to their Shirts, and drinking Bawdy-Healths." At one point Malagene plays the Jew's harp. Songs include love lyrics about shepherds and shepherdesses, a Scottish melody, a French tune, and an Irish croon. The dance most often mentioned and demonstrated is the *coranto,* but Caper and Saunter know all the new steps and seem congenitally incapable of standing still: at the end of the play Goodvile, maddened by all the frenetic merrymaking, has them hobbled and gagged by his footmen, and barnishes them from his house in dunce's caps. The remarkably choreographed confusion of this comedy is so dazzling it is hard to believe that it could have been devised by the same person who wrote *Alcibiades.* Otway mastered the lessons of Molière in timing and distraction and borrowed the minor-key cynicism of Wycherley, whose *Plain Dealer* had been produced in 1676 with vast success. Writing for the company of players with whose talents he was now thoroughly familiar, Otway would seem to have reached yet another height of achievement and versatility.

Still another display of acting deserves some special attention, the passage in the very heart of the plot when Mrs. Goodvile (Elizabeth Barry) "pretends" for Goodvile's sake to be carrying on a flirtation with Truman. Of course we know that she is in fact having an affair with Truman, but her staged flirtation is designed to enrage her husband in order that she may then "prove" that all was staged for the purpose of making him jealous—and thus persuade him of her innocence. To this end she conspires with Truman to "work him up to the heights of furious suspicion" and then "baffle him out of it." Goodvile returns to his own house in disguise with two masked ladies, hoping to surprise his wife with Truman. But his cast-off mistress Victoria, knowing of the plot, decides to take her revenge on him by forewarning Mrs. Goodvile, so the lady is prepared. Goodvile finds her in Truman's arms, boasting happily of her husband's indulgence in departing and leaving her "Mistress of such freedome . . . To spend my days in Triumph as I do, to Sacrifice my Self, my Soul, and all my Sense to you, the Lord of all my Joys, my Conqueror and Protector." But her greatest accomplishment is yet to follow, when she persuades Goodvile that this was all an act to make him suffer. She assumes an imperious rage in declaiming her innocence, concluding with the wish that "I might to your Torment perswade you still all your Jealousies were just, and I as Infamous as you are cruel," whereupon she stamps offstage in a fury. Goodvile is half-convinced by the display and turns to Truman with the feeble request, "If thou hast enjoyed her, I beg thee keep it close, and if it be possible let us yet be Friends."

This is obviously another showcase passage, written for the especial talents of Mrs. Barry. Tradition has it that after her first indifferent performance in 1674, Lord Rochester became her acting coach, instructing her particularly in stage diction and "cadence" to offset the flat monotone she had until then affected. She became renowned for her splendid voice and intelligent acting, so that Colley Cibber wrote of her that she had:

a presence of elevated dignity, her mien and motion superb, and gracefully majestick, her voice full, clear, and strong, so that no violence of passion could be too much for her; and when distress, or tenderness possessed her, she subsided into the most affecting melody and softness. In the art of exciting pity, she had a power beyond all the actresses I have yet seen, or what your imagination can conceive. . . . In scenes of anger, defiance, or resentment, while she was impetuous and terrible, she pour'd out the sentiment with an enchanting harmony.[1]

Flouncing off the stage in a fit of pique was sure to prompt a special burst of applause befitting her famous talent.

We should also remember here that the actress is the woman Otway both loved and resented so intensely that he had, at the time of this play's production, left the country with the army to forget her refusal to return his passion. The scene can be read as an interesting piece of personal revenge, for in his role as playwright Otway can force Mrs. Barry to "confess" the deceit he personally believed her capable of:

Now, once more let me invoke all the Arts of Affectation, all the Revenge, all the counterfeit Passions, pretended Love, pretended Jealousies, pretended Rage, and in sum the very Genius of my Sex to my assistance.

It is not too farfetched to assume a biographical intention. A look at the epilogue to this play, spoken by Barry, reminds us that the use of the words "luck" and "fortune" nearly always is a clue that Otway is writing about his personal circumstances. "Poets themselves their own ill luck have wrought" bespeaks his own dejection at this time.

From the Epistle Dedicatory, to the Earl of Dorset (later Lord Buckhurst), we learn that *Friendship in Fashion* was alleged to libel members of the court, for Otway ostentatiously denies any such intention. This is an example of his working "by contraries," as in the assurance to the ladies that there is no bawdy material to be found in the play. Whoever the fashionable people were who saw themselves caricatured in this play, we will never know. We do know, however, that Otway fell out of Buckhurst's favor soon thereafter, allegedly over sponsoring this play, and that he had to struggle for patrons for his next few plays. It is not to the court's credit that the drinking and whoring and affected posturing could be construed to apply to dozens of members of the aristocracy who revelled with the Merry Monarch: nor is it to their credit that they withdrew their support from a writer whose considerable talent made them recognize themselves. In any case, the charge of libel was more serious at the time that that of sexual indecency, but very shortly afterward, and for a long time to come thanks to the eventual triumph of the Whig Puritan ethic, these would be reversed.

Montague Summers passes on an interesting note concerning a revival of *Friendship in Fashion* at Drury Lane in 1749, as reported by Tate Wilkinson in *The Mirror, or, the Actor's Tablet*:

Be it noticed, Dame C. was not blessed with beauty—though of infinite talents; yet she unfortunately in that Comedy was ideally ravished twice or thrice before the fourth act ended which the audience very properly judged to be too much for that lady's feelings, and not knowing what might happen in the fifth, they consequently put a final and violent stop to all farther indecent proceedings.[2]

If this is true, the Georgian audience proved even more squeamish than Kitty Clive's Squeamish. The notorious Nicky-Nacky flagellation scenes had been cut from productions of *Venice Preserv'd* as early as 1718 and were not restored (except for special private productions) until the 1895 Paris performance of the play: the Puritan backlash had taken hold.

Jeremy Collier's *Short View of the Profaneness and Immorality of the English Stage* (1698) sets forth the Puritan objections to Restoration drama. He accuses comedy of "idealizing debauchery, and of rewarding an Atheistical Bully with a lady and a fortune."[3] The greatest emphasis in Collier's attack is upon atheism. He found that Chamont's abuse of the Chaplain in Otway's *The Orphan* was dangerously irreverent, and Monimia's bridal ecstasy he labeled "smutty" and profane.[4]

Later generations, of course, found the sexual license in these plays offensive for other than religious reasons, which is to be expected considering the broad social impact of the Whig Puritan revolution. The gradual canonization of the role of wife and mother to become "the angel in the home" by Victorian times indicates a social rather than a religious change. The very notion of a marriage between two sexual opportunists, like the Goodviles, is thoroughly unrespectable. And the fact that Mrs. Goodvile wins the skirmish in *Friendship in Fashion*, assuring her the right to pursue still further her own libertine instincts, is seen as nothing less than degenerate.

With the revival of interest in Restoration drama in the 1920s, one might expect to see the emergence of a critical attitude which differs from Collier's. This is not the case. Joseph Wood Krutch, in *Comedy and Conscience after the Restoration*, follows the Puritans in insisting that most Restoration comedy is simply obscene "unprintable" stuff which only pretends to scourge folly and vice while in fact titillating a jaded and decadent aristocracy.[5]

In his 1946 study of Restoration comedy, L. C. Knights points out that sexual indecency is nothing new, but it is rather a bore: "the criticism that defends of Restoration comedy need to answer is not that the comedies are 'immoral' but that they are trivial, gross, and dull."[6] *Friendship in Fashion* surely exposes the triviality of the preoccupations of its idle characters, and the amount and variety of the sexual entanglements are possibly offensive to some as being gross, not to mention some of the language and the "well-meaning hints," but the play could never be described as dull unless a five-ring circus is considered the apotheosis of tedium.

Eleven years after Knight, in 1957, Dale Underwood's study *Etherege and the Seventeenth Century Comedy of Manners* undertakes to interpret the serious philosophical bases of the libertine attitude. Writing of Etherege which might as well apply to Otway, Underwood observes:

If he saw the sterility of an idle leisure class devoted to pleasure and politesse, he also saw even as he worked valiantly in the midst of it, the sterility—the hypocrisy, cunning, pettiness, and amorality—in the traditionally worthier realms of man's endeavor and aspiration. . . . And there is no reason to suppose that he found the one world more noble and worthy and less comic than the other. Thus the fact that his plays offer no adequate alternative to the frivolity which they expose would seem to indicate for their author the final comedy of man.[7]

The Country Wife, The Plain Dealer, The Man of Mode, and *Friendship in Fashion* all appeared in a three-year period between 1675 and 1678. In each of these plays, the artificiality of the *beau monde* clashes with the "natural instincts" of man. Manly, the Plain Dealer, sets out to demonstrate the hypocrisy of society by stubbornly insisting upon saying what he thinks. Like Molière's *Misanthrope,* he proves that society cannot tolerate honesty.

Contempt for the institution of marriage is a convention in these plays. Where the game of courtship is played to the finish— marriage—rather than defaulting to seduction, we usually find that sex has been purchased in exchange for freedom, that love is a transitory madness from which married couples swiftly recover only to find themselves burdened and unhappily confined, like the disintegrating couple in Hogarth's *Marriage à la Mode.* Until recently, critics merely dismissed this convention as a symptom of the general immorality of Charles's reign, and looked no deeper. But Dale Underwood and subsequent scholars have argued that an interpretation of nature lies beneath the libertine philosophy. The urban life of fashion, like the created need for gold, is obviously unnatural. Natural creatures do not marry but mate—mating is natural, marriage unnatural. To take the traditional marriage vows with the intention of keeping true to them denies nature and runs counter to empirical observation. It is the duty of intelligent creatures to understand themselves as thoroughly as possible, and to survive in society, they necessarily must assume a

Machiavellian role and play social games while secretly protecting the freedom to pursue natural instincts. From this stems the tremendous caution we observe in the traditional Restoration pair who find themselves unattached, enlightened, and in love with each other. A sexual attraction for someone else's husband or wife may be seen as quite normal and easy to deal with, but finding oneself in love with another free person presents alarming difficulties. Otway underplays the courtship of Camilla and Valentine in his comedy, making them function as the sex objects who foil the respective lusts of Goodvile and Lady Squeamish, but he deals most extensively with the dilemma of honest lovers in his last comedy, *The Atheist.*

Friendship in Fashion is a Restoration orgy. Its premise is that everyone, given the leisure and privacy of a frolic in a moonlit garden, is a sexual opportunist at heart. This represents the antithesis of the stern Platonic chastity maintained at all costs in the heroic drama of the time. Even Roswell Gray Ham, Otway's most recent biographer, cannot understand how the poet could indulge in such base sensuality:

We may be certain that the nausea they (the comedies) raise in us was not unintentional from one who, as time proceeded, spoke with an increasing bitterness of the scurvy fortune that had plunged him into a world of scribbling fops and enameled women. One recalls the tenderly nurtured child beside the Rother stream, the mildly Puritan cast of his earliest education, and then turns to this latter portrait wherein the disillusioned sentimentalist gazes upon his creatures with disgust. The contrast worked itself out into the two worlds of tragedy and comedy. The one, with its Jaffeirs and Belvideras, was the embodiment of all that he ever dreamed of life; the other, with its Claras, Squeamishes, and Antonios, all that he saw.[8]

Despite the indulgent sentiment of Professor Ham's apology for Otway's "nauseating" comedies, when apology seems uncalled for, there is a peculiar kind of truth in these remarks. The cynicism of his first original comedy is in startling contrast to the idealism of his heroic plays. It is tempting to explain this by citing the biographical circumstances which might have induced new bitterness, such as the unrequited passion for Elizabeth Barry. If, however, we recall Lady Squeamish's cry for "tender, moving" tragedies with "vertuous ladies" as well as her hypocritical disgust with the new bawdiness in comedy, we might consider that this is what Otway assumes his audiences expect in each genre: he sees himself catering to popular taste.

Thus far, the world outside Drury Lane has not yet encroached upon his dramatic consciousness, but by the time he returns from Flanders with the partially written script of *Caius Marius,* his work reflects profound changes. Otway knew when he wrote *Don Carlos* that he was a competent, even gifted, playwright: he revelled in the praise and admiration of the king's circle. But the circumstances of the times, the pernicious allegations of the Popish Plot rumors and the desperate Whig efforts to remove James from succession, rocked the throne and the entire governing establishment so that the profession of playwright, or even soldier, was as precarious as that of monarch. Rumor-mongers and political agitators clamored for the attention of the public, and Otway began to absorb literary subject matter from the real world. As a result, the seven years remaining of his short life were preoccupied with "the Circumstances of my Condition, whose daily business must be daily Bread."[9]

Caius Marius

In *Alcibiades* (1675) and *Don Carlos* (1676) Otway portrayed kings faced with problems within the court—disloyal queens, evilly scheming advisers, problem sons—who were undone by their own human weaknesses such as susceptibility to flattery or sexual jealousy. But in *Caius Marius* (1679) all of society from senator to sheepherder is in a tumult of violence and fear created by the ambition and cruelty of the title character. Otway's source for the story was Plutarch's *Lives,* the last complete edition of North's translation having appeared in 1676. The Dryden translation "by several hands" was to appear between 1683–1686, during the years when great numbers of writers, Otway included, hastened to try a turn at translation in order to survive.

In this play, Otway has captured the unsettled atmosphere implicit in Plutarch's account, where the consulship of Rome seemed to change with the winds generated by one powerful warrior after another. The grim perseverance and superstition of Marius is drawn from this source as well. He is determined to win the consulship a seventh time because in his youth he caught an eagle's nest as it fell and found that it contained seven eggs. The brief but strange intrusion of Martha, a Syrian prophetess whose foreknowledge Marius respected so much that he had her carried about with him on a litter to all of his campaigns. The glimpse of exile in Otway's play, however, is a far cry from the hardships described by Plutarch: Otway devises an enchanted Forest of Arden atmosphere, while Plutarch's Marius could not escape his pursuers even while concealing himself in the chilly mire of a swamp.

It is difficult to fathom what inspired Otway also to graft Shakespeare's *Romeo and Juliet* onto such forbidding material, since Marius Junior in Plutarch is married to the daughter of an ally and is enthusiastically training to transcend his father, if that is possible to imagine, in tyranny and cruelty to those who oppose him. Otway's Marius Junior manages to be a loyal son and a tender lover as well, somewhat in the pattern of Don Carlos. Lavinia, his Juliet, is a resourceful girl who runs away from Rome by herself to join her husband in exile in the enchanted forest. Only when her father's troops have seized her and forced her to return to marry the newest consul, is she obliged to capitulate to the stratagem of the two-days' sleeping potion. She reminds us of Alcibiades' wife, Timandra, who followed her husband on foot to Sparta when she learned that he had defected. Lavinia soothes the weary old tyrant in exile with peaches and pomegranates and water from a crystal spring, for all the world like a damsel in a medieval romance. And it is she who has the last word when she arises from her drugged sleep beside the corpse of Marius junior, only to witness the additional horror of her father-in-law in the act of murdering her father.

> And see how well I am at last rewarded.
> All could not balance for the short-term'd
>   Life
> Of one old man: You have my Father butcher'd,
> The onely Comfort I had left on Earth.
> The Gods have taken too my Husband from me.
> See where he lies, your and my onely Joy.
> This Sword yet reeking with my Father's Gore,
> Plunge it into my Breast: plunge, plunge
>   it thus.

Recalling suddenly how Lavinia had saved his life in exile, Marius recognizes her suicide for the rebuke that it is to his excessive cruelty. To the immense disgust of the mortally wounded Sulpitius, the old tyrant repents the inflamed ambition which has ruined the happiness he might have had in his children.

Lovers of Shakespeare are invariably chagrined or amused by the reworkings of his plays which turned up during the Restoration, like Dryden's *All for Love* or the two versions of *The Tempest*. Otway's apology in the Prologue acknowledges the superiority of the original:

> Though much the most unworthy of the Throng,
> Our this-day's Poet fears h'has done him
>   wrong.
> Like greedy Beggars that steal Sheaves away,
> You'll find h'has rifled him of half a Play.
> Amidst this baser Dross you'll see it shine
> Most beautifull, amazing, and Divine.

But Shakespeare wrote in happier times, Otway claims. Now the "Cares" of the king and his "Nation's Fears" have silenced the songs of the Muses, and he can only wait for happier days to let his own "unbounded Fancy write." Otway does not intend, as some neo-Classical writers did, to "improve" Shakespeare by imposing the proprieties of the stage and the amenities of modern language upon the original. He frankly plagiarizes the love scenes between Romeo and Juliet and contracts it to serve as a secondary plot to his otherwise "drumming, trumpeting and fighting play."

In the epilogue, Otway notes that some of the audience may have come to the play "only for love of Underhill and Nurse Nokes," indicating once again his awareness of the talents of the company's actors. James, not Robert, Nokes is the comedian who was renowned for his performances in women's attire, and Otway *via* Shakespeare provided him with one of the most popular roles of his life. Nokes was, according to Montague Summers, "entirely homosexual."[10] In any case, his exuberant transvestitism carried the secondary plot and was so memorable that he was given another female part the same season in D'Urfey's *The Virtuous Wife*. Summers points out that he was already nicknamed "Nurse" Nokes for his performance of the Nurse in *The Fatal Jealousie* (1672), and "doubtless this suggested to Otway the idea that he should also play Lavinia's Nurse."[11] Underhill played Sulpitius, Otway's cynical and bloodthirsty version of Mercutio, a serious role requiring a sustained display of spleen and swordsmanship. Knowing the preferences of his audience, the playwright has deliberately drawn them to his play by offering them a touch of Shakespeare's "tender, moving" love, a glimpse of their favorite camp comedian, and even a musical interlude—not to mention several displays of the new moving scenery and a covey of vestal virgins in *dishabille* offering to sacrifice their lives for their country. To demonstrate the consul's cruelty he even brings onstage a saccharine child actor, "a very harmless little boy," to plead "with my little dying hands" for the life of his beloved grandfather. Marius' reply must have provoked hisses:

> Take hence this Brat too; mount it on a Spear
> And let it sprawl to make the Grandsire sport.

He later relents and spares the child but not the old man.

We have noted already some of the Whig tactics which are reworked in terms of Roman history in this play, such as abuses of election procedure, false appeals to democracy and liberty, and mob violence. *Caius Marius* is the account of the fall of a tyrant whose ambition for a seventh consulship led Rome to new depths of corruption and violence. Dedicated pointedly to King Charles "the Lord of Hearts, and President of Wit," the play opens with offstage howls for "Liberty! Liberty! Marius and Sulpitius! Liberty! Liberty! Liberty!" Metellus, a man of probity and concern for his country's honor, deplores Marius' power over the people and determines that they must "check this Havocker, / That with his Kennell of the Rabble hunts / Our Senate into Holes and frights our Laws." Marius, for his part, ruminates upon the resistance of the Sylla-Metellus party, which he views as conspiring to prevent him from his rightful rule of the country he has served and defended in battle for forty years. Self-pityingly he asks, speaking of Rome, "Why does she use me thus?" His son offers an interpretation of the situation:

> Because she's rul'd
> By lazy Drones that feed on others Labours,
> And fatten with the fruits they never toil'd
>   for;
> Old gouty Senatours of crude Minds and Brains,
> That always are fermenting Mischief up,
> And style their private Malice publick Safety.

Old Marius had even twice proposed a marriage between his son and Metellus' daughter Lavinia, as a political gesture of appeasement, but he had been turned down. Young Marius suffers visibly at the mention of Lavinia's name, and he confesses his love for the girl who is "as harmless as the Turtle of the Woods." But his father is determined that the battle lines be drawn: "Let not a Hair of that Metellus scape thee, / Who'd strip my Age of its most dear bought Honours." Young Marius, like Don Carlos, is loyal to his father and agrees sadly never to speak Lavinia's name again.

In the second act, which is more Shakespeare's than Otway's, we learned that Lavinia reciprocates young Marius' love, though her father wants her to marry Sylla. Sylla plans to enter Rome and take the consulship the next morning, but Marius Junior and Lavinia have a few moments of conversation in the garden. "O Marius, Marius! Wherefore art thou Marius?" This is hardly a distortion of Shakespeare, for Otway sensibly refuses to alter the original for the most part, but Fielding chose this line to mock in his *Tom Thumb*: "O, Tom Thumb! Tom Thumb! Wherefore art thou Tom Thumb?" A footnote refers us to "Otway's Marius." "There's such sweet pain in parting," says Marius Junior, altering the familiar line. Otway's condensation removes a good deal of the leisurely and sensuous love poetry, like Romeo's swearing by the moon "that tips with silver all these fruit-tree tops." But with few exceptions, the borrowed passages leave Shakespeare's language intact.

The second act concludes with a brawl in the Forum resulting from the debate between Marius and Metellus. A mob has been mustered to voice its support of Marius: "Marius! Marius! Marius! No Sylla! No Sylla! No Sylla!" Marius claims to hold the affection of the citizenry because of his humble birth. "I care not for a Lord: what good do they doe? nothing but run in our debts, and ly with our Wives," claims one of the citizens. Marius assures them that he loves the liberties and laws of Rome, as well as the rights and privileges of the free-born Romans, but just as he is about to be presented with the symbols of consulship Metellus interrupts the proceedings. In a sixteen-line speech Metellus claims that Marius is a tyrant who will enslave the people, seize their estates, and claim their wives. It will serve them right, he adds, "Such Slaves, who sell their Charters for a Holiday." Absurdly, the fickle mob begins to shout, "No Marius! No Marius!" Metellus instructs Quintus

Pompeius to declare Marius a traitor, Sulpitius and his henchmen draw swords, and the fracas begins.

Sulpitius murders Pompeius, and his guards subdue the crowd by force. Marius reveals his true feelings about the free-born Romans he has just claimed to love:

> These Slaves,
> These wide-mouth'd Brutes that bellow thus
>   for Freedome,
> Oh! how they ran before the hand of Pow'r,
> Flying for shelter into every Brake!
> Like cow'rdly fearful Sheep they break their
>   Herd,
> When the Wolf's out, and ranging for his Prey.

He frees all the slaves who will agree to support him against Sylla, and assigns the task of enforcing his victory to Sulpitius.

There can be no question that Otway is speaking as a Royalist of 1679 in his depiction of the Roman power struggle. Sulpitius and Granius speak as Tories in their opinion that Marius should have destroyed all his enemies while he had the opportunity, for "Mercy but gives Sedition time to rally":

> Ev'ry soft, pliant, talking, busy Rogue,
> Gathering a Flock of hot-brain'd Fools
>   together,
> Can preach up new Rebellion. Till the Heads
> Of all those heavn'ly inspired Knaves be
>   crush'd,
> No Power can be safe . . .

In this passage the language plainly indicates that Otway's thoughts are on the Puritan Whigs of his own day, who unlike the Romans claimed heavenly inspiration in "preaching" rebellion to their "flocks." The "Mercy" indicated alludes to Charles's apparent indifference to the Pope-burners and supporters of Monmouth. The Tories disapproved of his permissiveness wholeheartedly and pressed constantly for harsh and swift retribution for such examples of sedition. Marius in this scene reveals that he finds such harsh measures difficult:

> I have a tender Foolishness within me
> May sometimes get the better of my Rage:
> Sulpitius, therefore keep me warm; still
>   ply
> My ebbing Fury with the Thoughts of Sylla,
> Th'ungratefull Senate, and Metellus Pride;
> And let not any thing may make me dreadfull
> Be left undone.

This admission prepares us for the final scene of the play when Marius realizes that he has gone too far in cruelty and repents, much to Sulpitius' disgust. Sulpitius' tactic is always to "keep the Fools hot":

> Preach Dangers in their Ears,
> Spread false Reports o' th' Senate, working
>   up
> Their Madness to a Fury quick and desp'rate,
> Till they run headlong into civil Discords,
> And doe our business with their own Destruction.

He is a model of Whig propagandist and agitator.

Sylla and his troops are welcomed as deliverers, as Monmouth was, when they return to Rome. In the dialogue between Sylla and Marius which precedes their battle, the issue resolves once again to a matter of Marius' lowly birth. Marius declares that if Sylla had been born a peasant instead of a lord, he would remain a peasant, but he, Marius, in his glorious defense of Rome, earned his high renown. Otway chooses to emphasize class struggle here although it is only incidental in Plutarch, suggesting that he sees this story as a paradigm for the contemporary situation. It is Marius' ingratitude to Metellus, who "rais'd thee from a Peasant to a Lord" which Sylla finds offensive, while Marius accuses Sylla of deviousness in his ascent to power.

When the two sides fight, Marius is defeated. Quintus Pompeius banishes him from Rome, whereupon he falls to his knees and sarcastically thanks the gods for his fortune, then joins hands with his men and swears upon the Infernal powers to bring destruction on the city: "Let not one Stone of all her Tow'rs stand safe. Let not her Temples nor her Gods escape. Let Husbands in their Wives Embraces perish. Her Young Men massacred, Her Virgins ravisht." The ignominy of defeat seems to have succeeded in hardening his heart at last, but he is unaware that the curse of destruction he invokes will include the ruin of his own family.

Lavinia and Marius share the last night before exile, in a scene that is Shakespeare's and not Otway's. When Marius departs to join his father, however, Lavinia decides to follow him, escapes her nurse, and finds her way to Salonium.

Salonium ("the Country") is inhabited by curiously English rustics who interpret the "sad times" by means of natural signs. "Nay," says one good fellow, "I thought there was no good Weather towards, when my bald-fac'd Heifer stuck up her Tail Eastward, and ran back into a new Quick-set, which I had just made to keep the Swine from the Beans." Soldiers appear, pursuing Marius to kill him and ransack his home, and he is obliged to hide in the woods and eavesdrop while the men who once served under his command discuss how they will kill him. In Plutarch, Caius Marius dashes into a swamp and covers himself with rushes and mud, where he is captured nonetheless.

The arrival of Lavinia, who has been lost until she spotted her name carved in an oak tree, transforms the whole situation. Old Marius learns that she is his son's wife, and gently summons her to him for his blessing. She offers him a dainty picnic as well as some gold and jewels she had brought along. A joyful reunion with young Marius follows, Otway's rather than Shakespeare's.

> In these Woods,
> Whilst from pursuing Enemies you're safe,
> I'll range about and find the Fruits and
>   Springs,
> Gather cool Sedges, Daffadills and Lillies,
> And softest Camomil to make us Beds,
> Whereon my Love and I at night will sleep,
> And dream of better Fortune.

Absurd as this is, considering the rest of the play, it attempts to express Otway's belief in the transfiguring power of love: the forest seems safe and enchanted. Even Old Marius, "sitting in Sorrow on the naked Earth," utterly stripped of power and wealth, is treated to a gentle peal of soft music. It is his favorite prophetess, the Syrian Martha, who coincidentally has inhabited these woods ever since she was banished from Rome for serving him. She advises him that Cinna too has been banished from the city and is coming to seek him out so that they may establish a coalition which will return and reclaim Rome. Then with a wave of her wand, she gives the old man some sleep while a dance is performed. So powerful is the enchantment at this moment that even a hired assassin who appears suddenly on the scene is unable to kill the sleeping tyrant. This detail, bereft of magic, is drawn from Plutarch: he reports that a barbarian sent to murder Marius suffered an amazing change of heart, dropped his sword and cried, "I cannot kill Caius Marius!"

In very short order Lavinia disappears, Sulpitius appears, and Cinna arrives. Marius Senior and his sons arm themselves and march off to seize Rome. Obviously too much has happened in "the Country" to be managed in a scene only three hundred lines long, for this episode to be accepted as plausible. Otway is experimenting here with a dreamlike suspension of reality which imports psychological truth rather than rational experience—some would say unsuccessfully. This scene tries to portray some paradoxes of fortune. Fortune's wheel has cast the old tyrant down as far as he has ever fallen, and yet he finds that he has two loyal sons and a daughter-in-law whose loving ministrations restore his life. The Syrian prophetess marks with her appearance, the sudden improvement in his fortune. Fate and Fortune are alluded to nine times in this scene, always in the sense of a whimsical power which is beyond human control. Lavinia describes herself as "a poor unhappy Woman, driven by Fortune," but when Marius calls her his daughter she rejoices: "I'm much o'repaid for all the Wrongs of Fortune." Martha reminds Marius that she used to "wait upon thee with good Fortune," though since her departure he claims that all his good Fortune has left him. And when Cinna and Sulpitius arrive to ask Marius to lead them back to Rome, he feels that the turn of the Wheel is complete:

> For that fair Mistriss Fortune, which has cost
> So dear, for which such Hardships I have past,
> Is coy no more, but crowns my Hopes at last.
> I long t'embrace her, nay, 'tis Death to stay.

We know from *The Poet's Complaint* that Otway broods a good deal on the seductions and betrayals of Dame Fortune, whom he compares to a strumpet, and in this play we can observe the development of his metaphor. He interprets Plutarch's account of the turbulent career of Marius as proof of the vagaries of life's circumstances. The old tyrant is incensed by the ingratitude of his people—his soldiers attack him when he is out of power, his tenants forget him, and the country he has made glorious banishes him. As superstitious as his own herdsmen, he trusts dreams and prophecies to determine his action, hoping always for some insight into his future. And yet when he is most at the mercy of the elements, he is most safe, because of the gratuitous love and loyalty of his children.

The fifth act is a savage return to realism. Marius' vengeful return to Rome is interspersed with the deaths of the young lovers, culminating in the scene in the tomb. Caius Marius' rage is exclusively focused upon the ingratitude of his people:

> When Fears are on them, then their kindest
> > Wishes
> And best Rewards attend the gallant Warriour:
> But Dangers vanisht, infamous Neglect,
> Ill Usage and Reproach are all his portion . . .

He arranges for Sulpitius to murder on the spot everyone he chooses to smile upon: still he recognizes his own desperation.

> Oh! can the Matrons and the Virgins Cries,
> The Screams of dying Infants, and the Groans
> Of murther'd men be Musick to appease me?
> Sure Death's not far from such a desp'rate Cure.

Unlike a comparable figure in a standard heroic play, Marius is not entirely deranged by his passion. He prays to the gods that his assault on Rome will resemble a violent storm, after which, "having no more Fury left in store, / Heav'ns face grows clear, the Storm is heard no more, / And Nature smiles as gaily as before." We are to assume that the old warrior hopes to restore peace and order through the paradoxical means of war and chaos, for he still believes, in spite of the experience in the enchanted forest of Salonium, that he can manipulate the affairs of men.

In the ensuing bloodbath we see children, old men and virgins abused and slaughtered in the name of Marius' revenge, as his contempt for the populace reaches its height. His eloquent address to a now-cringing Senate evokes all the deepest passions stirred up by the Popish Plot:

> False are your Safeties when indulg'd by Pow'r:
> For soon ye fatten and grow able Traitours.
> False are your Fears, and your Afflictions falser:
> For they cheat you, and make you hope for Mercy,
> Which you shall never gain at *Marius'* hands.
> Who trusts your Penitence is more than Fool.
> Rebellion will renew: ye can't be honest.
> Y'are never pleas'd but with the Knaves that
>   cheat you,
> And work your Follies to their private ends.
> For your Religion, like your Cloaths you wear it,
> To change and turn just as the Fashion alters.

We hear a new poetic voice in this ringing passage, a direct and powerful declamation against the Exclusion Crisis mobs, the "wide-mouth'd brutes that bellow thus for Freedome."

In the final scene, while Shakespeare's words attend the death of Marius Junior and the reviving of Lavinia from her potion, old Marius pursues Lavinia's father into the tomb and murders him before his daughter's eyes. With amazing composure, Lavinia reminds her father-in-law of their sojourn in the forest, and his rage dissolves in the recollection of her compassion and mercy toward him. "And see how well I am at last rewarded," she chides. Having neither the joy of her husband nor the comfort of her father remaining, she stabs herself with old Marius' sword. Remorse overtakes him and transforms him totally.

> Oh! let me bury Me and all my Sins
> Here with this good old man. Thus let me kiss
> Thy pale sunk Cheeks, embalm thee with my Tears . . .
> We might have all bin Friends, and in one House
> Enjoy'd the Blessings of eternal Peace.
> But oh! my cruel Nature has undone me.

This is the sort of extravagant emotion for which Otway became most renowned for the next two centuries, until it was condemned as sentimentality. That Marius should kiss the man he had just murdered, and then piteously, even childishly, complain that "we might have all bin Friends," can seem to be ridiculously out of proportion, as inappropriate as his quaint, somewhat Elizabethan warning that "ambition is a Lust that's never quencht." Sulpitius, like Pierre in *Venice Preserv'd*, does not recant and is not contrite: "A Curse on all Repentance! how I hate it! I'd rather hear a Dog howl than a Man whine."

It is not difficult to understand why critics have given *Caius Marius* short shrift. It is an extremely unruly play for an era that professed to revere the stately declamation of Racine. But Otway's "Drumming, Trumpetting, and Fighting Play" does not presume to be a masterpiece, as he admits in his epilogue. The playwright needs "ready Money for's Debenture," as he explains: "This Play came forth, in hopes his Friends would come / To help a poor Disbanded Souldier home."

In reexamining the prologue with its homage to Shakespeare, we note that Otway also points to two Roman poets, Ovid and Horace. "Ovid's soft Genius and his tender Arts / Of moving Nature melted hardest Hearts." Lady Squeamish's call for the "soft melting tender things" in tragedy may explain the final saccharine appeal to pity of the old tyrant. But Horace's "lofty Genius boldlier rear'd / His manly head," Otway says, so that he "lasht with a true Poet's fearless Rage / The Villainies and Follies of the Age." Indeed the new element in *Caius Marius* is the direct yet eloquent strain of Otway's "Horatian" voice, brutally assessing the "dark disorders of a divided state." The blending of the soft Genius with the lofty Genius requires a dramatic context considerably less confining than the usual heroic dilemma-oriented play. For a model Otway looks to Shakespeare, whom Dryden would accuse of "carelessness" and "a Lethargy of thought," for permission to stray from the classical unities and the rigors of rhymed couplets.

A review of the development of Otway's drama to this point reveals him to be an able student, though not yet an original genius. *Don Carlos* he recognized to be as good an example of the heroic play as he could bring forth, in particular exemplary for its capacity to move the audience to tears of pity. Molière and Racine gave him experience in editing and digesting longer works, as well as an opportunity to rework some of the classical devices of the *commedia dell'arte* in the first case, and the sustenance of "grand" and stately sentiment in the latter. Wycherley and Etherege taught him the mode of libertine cynicism, which he carried daringly into the realm of serious drama. But he alone found his "Horatian" voice upon returning destitute to London from Flanders, to discover for himself the terrible effects of the political upheaval pursuant to the Popish Plot. At the age of twenty-seven, after six years of pursuing his Muse within the ivory tower of the company of actors he had come to understand so well, the violent struggle embodied in the Exclusion Crisis reached his sensibilities as deeply as they touched his pocketbook. A Royalist by temperament, deeply moved by the ideals of chivalry, he longed for the support and respect of "a gracious Prince's Favour . . . a constant Favour he ne'er feared to lose." His reappraisal of life, elucidated in *The Poet's Complaint of His Muse,* reflects the deepest moral contradictions of the times. But his resolution to have the ear of the heads of state, as Horace had his Maecenas, brought him no reward, for the ever-dwindling potential patrons were themselves too enmeshed in the current crisis to grant safe harbor to poets.

The Orphan

The Orphan, appearing in late February or early March 1680, is the most domestic of Otway's original tragedies. Perhaps for this reason—and because of its reputation for "moving mightily"—it held the stage for the next 125 years, along with *Venice Preserv'd.* Elizabeth Barry was the consummate orphan of the title. Her sympathy and affiliation with the role was so great that she supposedly told Gildon that "she never pronounced those three words in The Orphan, Ah! poor Castalio! without tears."[12] She "owned" the role, and played it for twenty-seven years. Thomas Betterton, who like Mrs. Barry had appeared in all of Otway's plays to date, played the unhappy Castalio. A young actor, Joseph Williams, played the libertine character of Polydore: it is relevant that he had also played the skeptical Don John of Austria in *Don Carlos.* All told, there are eleven characters in *The Orphan,* compared to eighteen in *Caius Marius* (not counting the mobs and guards, virgins, old men, and ruffians in the latter). Most of the action turns upon Monimia, her suitors Castalio and Polydore, their father Acasto, and her brother Chamont.

Charles Gildon, in his *Art of Poetry* (1718) and *Laws of Poetry* (1721), is perhaps most responsible for the critical exaltation of Otway's tragic genius in the first half of the eighteenth century. It was Gildon who found perfect adherence to the unities in *The Orphan*:

Indeed we have few Plays free from this absurdity [of underplots], of which *The Orphan* is one, and every Episode, Part or Under-Action, carries on and contributes to the main Action or Subject.[13]

Aline Mackenzie Taylor traces the history of Otway's reputation as a playwright who ranked for years in the popular imagination as "next to Shakespeare" in her book of the same title. She points to Pope's official sanction of this association in his *Epistle to Augustus*:

> Not but the tragic spirit was our own,
> And full in Shakespeare, fair in Otway shone.

This yoking of Otway's name with Shakespeare's became a critical reflex and cliché over the hundred years from Pope's *Epistle* to Hallam's *Introduction to the Literature of Europe* (1837). Even Doctor Johnson's reservations (1779) did not stifle the association; not until Shakespeare's star rose in the nineteenth century did Otway's begin to wane. Interestingly, Taylor suggests that the demise of his reputation might finally be blamed on "the emphasis on reading plays as though they were non-dramatic pieces" which "brought to light many of the forgotten Elizabethans; how many of the established favorites it helped to kill must be a matter of conjecture."[14]

The Orphan is a fine example of a play which cannot stand up very well to literary analysis, though in theatrical terms its sweep of action and emotion is preeminently successful. Many readers have been bemused by Mrs. Barry's involuntary tears at the line "Ah! poor Castalio!" Even more have been puzzled over Monimia's darkened bedchamber, which precluded her recognizing that she was making love to her husband's twin brother. Apart from the absence of a candle, literal minded readers have wondered why Castalio, the bridegroom, did not confide his marriage to the brother to whom he was quite devoted. And even more sophisticated—or jaded—readers have wondered why this sexual misadventure could not have been resolved later instead of precipitating the tragic deaths of all three principal characters. But readers of a play have the leisure to ponder such matters: a reader of *Oedipus,* one of the plays in Otway's mind when he wrote *The Orphan,* might well wonder why Jocasta, knowing the prophecy, would not only marry a man young enough to be her son, but a man with bad feet. When one submits to the "willing suspension of disbelief" required by the theater, however, such matters must stand aside while the pattern of feeling and action creates the special illusions necessary. Otway is far from *Alcibiades* and its wooden declamation; he has become adept at maintaining complex action while sustaining the "mighty line."

The plot of *The Orphan* is relatively simple. Acasto, a former courtier, has taken his household to the country in order to protect his family from the hypocrisy and corruption of the court. His twin sons, Castalio and Polidore, have studied hunting instead of the arts of war and politics, but they are at an age when they resent their father's protec-tiveness and long to find out for themselves what life is truly like. The twins have both fallen in love with Monimia, the orphan of the title, who has grown up with them as Acasto's ward. At the beginning of the play they decided to court her and agree to let her choose between them. They are as ignorant of love as they are of battle, but here also they are eager to learn. Monimia is in love with Castalio, however, and she marries him secretly. Observing her closely with his brother, Polidore concludes that she must be a whore. Therefore he determines to intrude upon what is in fact his brother's wedding night, feeling certain that if Monimia was willing to arrange to spend the night with Castalio, she must be "fair game" for him as well.

He arrives first at her bedchamber and claims Monimia: Castalio then is kept out by the maidservant who believes him to be Polidore. The next morning, Monimia is bewildered by Castalio's cruel abuse of her until the situation is discovered. Polidore learns that Monimia is his brother's wife, and tragedy closes in. He and Monimia are overcome with shame and remorse. The embittered, still unenlightened Castalio concludes that women are cruel and irrational creatures. Monimia tries but cannot bring herself to explain to him specifically what has hap-pened to distress her so much: she only mystifies him further by vowing to go to some faraway place to waste her life in misery. Polidore than arrives and deliberately calls Monimia a whore, so that Castalio will kill him, and he does. Dying, Polidore thanks his brother and explains how

his lust has polluted Castalio's marriage bed. Monimia poisons herself.
Polidore reveals that she was completely innocent of any complicity in
the crime. Cursing his stars, Castalio runs himself through with his
sword.

This is the essence of the action. There are two other characters of
importance, Acasto the recluse and Monimia's brother Chamont.
Chamont has come to the country retreat out of a strange sense of
foreboding. An old crone has warned him to "hasten to save a Sister"
from being dishonored by Castalio and Polidore, and he has also had a
prophetic dream about Monimia being caressed by two wanton lovers.
Suddenly awakening from the nightmare, he leaped out of his bed,
seized his sword to attack the phantom, and then:

> I found my weapon had the arras pierc'd,
> Just where that famous tale was interwoven,
> How th'unhappy *Theban* slew his Father.

Otway's allusion to *Oedipus* provides a warning of what is to come as
well as carrying with it all the associative horrors of incest. In order to
experience this play as a tragedy, Monimia's rape by her brother-in-law
must be seen as a violation of the taboo against incest. Chamont's most
important fuction in the play is to sustain the audience's fear for
Mionimia's chastity through his own intense concern for her honor. Just
when we all might be most satisifed that marriage vows have at last
insured the orphan's protection, we find Castalio refused admittance to
the bedchamber where his brother is making love to his wife.

The situation recalls Otway's angry letter to Elizabeth Barry in
which he draws the conclusion that she had turned him away from her
door because she was entertaining a lover: "I cannot bear the thought of
being made a Property either of another Man's good Fortune, or the
Vanity of a Woman that designs nothing but to plague me."[15] Another
of his letters concludes, "Remember poor Otway." Surely nothing
could keep his memory so alive as this scene from *The Orphan*. With
each of the ten revivals of this popular tragedy, for twenty-two years
after his death until she was well into her middle years, the actress
relived her betrayal of "poor Castalio."

The figure of Acasto closely resembles that of Belarius, the banished
lord in Shakespeare's *Cymbeline*.[16] He is deeply disillusioned with the
court he once served and devotes much of his time to explaining the

vanity and hypocrisy of the world to the children he has carefully
isolated from it. Like Guiderius and Arviragus in *Cymbeline,* Polidore
and Castalio want to join the army, but Acasto forbids them to do it:

> You'll find
> Corruption, envy, discontent, and Faction,
> Almost in every Band: how many men
> Have spent their bloud in their dear Countries
>   service,
> Yet now pine under want, while selfish slaves,
> That ev'n would cut their throats, whom now
>   they fawn on,
> Like deadly Locusts eat the Honey up,
> Which those industrious Bees so hardly toyl'd
>   for.

Acasto retains his deep loyalty to the king, despite the evil world that
surrounds his power. When his sons convince him that their only wish
is to serve their king, he promises that someday they shall have their
chance: "Yes, my aspiring Boys, / Ye shall have business when your
Master wants you, / You cannot serve a nobler." Otway will not be
found guilty of treason here.

As long as he can be persuaded that his sons are not likely to become
fawning courtiers, seeking favors and preferments, Acasto will let them
go. For though his disillusionment is profound, his love for the king has
never wavered. His view of life compares neatly to Otway's own in *The
Poet's Complaint* of the same year, but his habit of giving advice recalls
Polonius:

> Avoid the politick, the factious Fool,
> The busie, buzzing, talking, hardn'd Knave;
> The quaint, smooth Rogue, that sins against
>   his Reason;
> Calls sawcy loud Suspicion, publick Zeal,
> And Mutiny the dictates of his spirit.

This is the voice of an old Cavalier who sees nothing but self-interest
and malicious mischief underlying the Whig cause.

On the subject of religion, he advises:

> If y'ave Religion, keep it to your selves,
> Atheists will else make use of Toleration,
> And laugh ye out on't; never shew Religion
> Except ye mean to pass for Knaves of Conscience,
> And cheat believing Fools that think ye honest.

This speech is made to his entire household, including his Chaplain. Jeremy Collier, who attacked Chamont's ruthless interrogation of this same Chaplain as indicating Otway's disrespect for the clergy, did not remark upon Acasto's cynicism in this passage, though he certainly might have found it useful as ammunition.

In the same speech Acasto advises his sons against marriage. The audience knows that Castalio and Monimia have just exchanged vows before the Chaplain in the grove. "Let Marriage be the last mad thing ye doe, / For all the Sins and Follies of the past." The old patriarch's injunction against matrimony serves to reinforce the secrecy which the lovers find necessary at that moment. Acasto is making this speech because he is ill and fears that he may not have long to live, so possibly concern for his fragile health underlies the concealment of the marriage. Certainly Monimia fears awakening Acasto, whose room is next to hers, for she agrees to see her husband for their wedding-night only if he promises to be extremely quiet. Much critical attention has been given to this problem of secrecy: why couldn't Castalio announce his marriage at this gathering of the family, then ask for his father's blessing and his brother's forgiveness? Most likely Acasto's speech is the very factor which restrains him. After a harsh assessment of the world's duplicity and injunction against the folly of marrying, the moment is not opportune.

Acasto's opinions on life provide the only guide to experience that the twins have ever known, and we can see in each of them a tendency to philosophize which they have absorbed from their disappointed father. Polidore in particular has developed a habit of sententious rationalization. He woos Monimia, for example, with a theory on the origins of language:

> Desire first taught us words: Man, when
>   created
> At first alone, long wander'd up and down,
> Forlorn, and silent as his vassal Beasts;

> But when a heav'n-born Maid, like you, appear'd,
> Strange pleasures fill'd his eyes, and fir'd his
>   heart,
> Unloos'd his Tongue, and his first talk was Love.

But she does not reciprocate his love and when she tells him so, he
further rationalizes his feelings of insult and anger:

> Who'd be that sordid foolish thing call'd man,
> To cringe thus, fawn, and flatter for a pleasure,
> Which Beasts enjoy so very much above him?
> The lusty Bull ranges through all the Field,
> And from the herd singling his Female out,
> Enjoyes her, and abandons her at will.

Polidore's libertinism is not the result of exposure to the fashionable
attitudes of the day, but is drawn from his own firsthand observations of
nature. When he studies the happiness of Monimia and his brother, not
comprehending its source, he concludes sourly that she is a whore.
Once again he rationalizes in terms of beasts and hunters:

> Half to compliance brought by me, surpriz'd
> Her sinking Vertue till she yielded quite,
> So Poachers basely pick up tir'd Game,
> Whilst the fair Hunter's cheated of his Prey.

Therefore on the wedding-night, when Polidore comes to the bedchamber before Castalio does, he has persuaded himself that he is only
enjoying his rightful prey. Imagery of the hunt pervades *The Orphan*.
Our introduction to the twins shows them returning breathless from an
encounter with a wild boar who had knocked Castilio down. Polidore
had risked his own life jumping from a precipice to aid his brother in
the struggle.

When Castalio is kept out of the bedchamber by the maid who
believes him to be Polidore, his anger turns on his wife: "Sure now
sh'has bound me fast, and means to Lord it, / To rein me hard, and ride
me at her will." He too catches the infection of philosophy and delivers
a bitter denunciation of the female sex which fulfills Otway's own threat
to Mrs. Barry to "as often as I henceforth think of you, curse Womankind for ever."[17]

> Woman the Fountain of all Humane Frailty!
> What mighty ills have not been done by Woman?
> Who was't betrayed the Capitol? A Woman.
> Who lost Mark Anthony the World? A Woman.
> Who was the cause of a long ten years War,
> And laid at last Old Troy in Ashes? Woman.
> Destructive, damnable, deceitful Woman.

He pursues this line of reasoning with an interpretation of the fall of man:

> Woman to Man first as a Blessing giv'n,
> When Innocence and Love were in their prime,
> Happy a while in Paradise they lay,
> But quickly Woman long'd to go astray,
> Some foolish new Adventure needs must prove,
> And the first Devil she saw she chang'd her
>   Love,
> To his Temptations lewdly she inclin'd
> Her soul, and for an Apple damn'd Mankind.

The parallel implied between Eden and Acasto's retreat here is significant. The sheltered brothers, innocent of the ways of the world, are nonetheless capable of evil. Monimia contrasts with Eve, however, in her perfect innocence: she is the ideal outlined by Lady Squeamish's injunction to "let your ladies be vertuous and say tender, moving things." Throughout the play she literally does nothing but react to situations that others have devised. Hers is a diapason of tender emotions, sometimes shifting quickly, but always in response. Monimia initiates no action at all—she simply amplifies the feelings inspired by the deeds of others. Not until she drinks poison in the last act does she do anything decisive, and many critics have found her total passivity and innocence the finest feature of the play.

Since the trend toward *tragedie larmoyante* or "weeping tragedy" was budding, Monimia's pitiful passivity was somewhat avant-garde. None of Otway's heroines to date had been quite so astoundingly helpless. Even Lavinia, his Juliet, showed more pluck than her Shakespearean model by following her husband into exile and, in the final scene, upbraiding her father-in-law for his cruelty. Some of Lavinia's extravagant fantasies about the horrors of the tomb are echoed in the passage where Monimia and Polidore make a pact of wretchedness, vowing to banish themselves, to "study to be unhappy / And find out ways to increase affliction." If a child should be born of this act, Monimia says, killing it would not be enough: they must let it live, knowing that their infamous deed will blight its life. Polidore agrees, adding:

> Let's find some place where Adders nest in Winter,
> Loathsome and Venomous; where poisons hang
> Like Gums against the Walls; where Witches meet
> By night and feed upon some pampered Imp,
> Fat with the Blood of Babes.

The imaginative excesses of this passage suggest, intentionally or not, the adolescent level of these characters.

Castalio, still oblivious to the reasons for his rejection the previous night, begins to rationalize his bitterness. He professes to envy the deer, who mate only once a year, and complains of love that "only the Beast of Reason is its Slave, / And in that Folly drudges all the year." Despite his anger, he is persuaded to attend Monimia when her maid summons him. Though Monimia makes a great effort, she cannot bring herself to explain to him what has transpired. Her hysteria and vague threats only baffle him, and she departs with the cry, "Ah poor Castalio!"

In his unhappiness and confusion Castalio turns to his brother for comfort, confessing the secret marriage at last and apologizing for having deceived him. But Polidore has apparently turned against him, too, though it is in fact his ulterior plan to goad Castalio into killing him. He achieves this by calling Monimia a whore and Castalio a coward. Then, mortally wounded, Polidore explains all while Monimia falters onto the scene, dying from the poison she has taken. Castalio invites the surviving members of his family to "come joyn with me and curse." "What?" asks Chamont, and Castalio replies:

> First thy self,
> As I do, and the hour that gave thee birth:
> Confusion and disorder seize the World,
> To spoyl all trust and converse amongst men;
> 'Twixt Families ingender endless fewds,
> In Countrys needless fears, in Cities factions,
> In States Rebellion, and in Churches Schism:

Till all things move against the course of Nature;
Till Form's dissolv'd, the Chain of Causes broken,
And the Originals of Being lost.

It is impossible to miss the specifically topical elements in this passage, the factions, rebellions, and schism, grafted onto the conventional concluding diatribe of heroic drama.

There is a softness about *The Orphan* that leads critics to accuse it of blatant sentimentality. Otway's admiration for *King Lear, Othello,* and *Romeo and Juliet* draws him toward the personal tragedy, making this the sort of play that John Cunningham criticizes for failing to show the "struggle between man and larger powers outside him."[18]

The stage history of *The Orphan* reveals a gradual and ultimately devastating pruning of the most bitter passages. We must reconsider Otway's careful preparation for Castalio's curse upon the universe, if the play is to be redeemed from the charge of excessive personal sentiment. The twins have been deliberately removed from civilization because Acasto determined to protect them from corruption. Their only active experience of life has been hunting, and we have seen that they are inclined to compare their pursuit of Monimia to their experience as predators. Further knowledge of the world outside the refuge is limited to what their father has told them, and his habitually cynical and embittered accounts of human depravity have been absorbed into their own philosophy of life, such as it is. Acasto has inadvertently destroyed the Eden he has tried to create, simply by his example. Both brothers are quick to assume the worst in any situation, even when their experience scarcely warrants such pessimism. Reason is their nemesis, and their natural affection and sense of loyalty is swiftly altered when they mimic their father's habit of rationalizing.

Eliminating Acasto's lengthy explanations of his disillusionment has the effect of sentimentalizing the play. He becomes merely a sickly but loving old man. Polidore becomes a contemptible lecher and Castalio, like Monimia, becomes a hapless victim. The whole foundation of their isolated existence becomes meaningless, and the rape itself becomes a revolting criminal act precipitating a pitiful, but not tragic, series of consequences. This may be what the eighteenth century wanted, however, in place of a moral framework which so explicitly challenges, like Sophocles' *Oedipus,* the beloved notion of free will.

The Soldier's Fortune

The Soldier's Fortune was first performed in the spring of 1680. There is a record of the king's attending a performance of this comedy on the first of March of that year. The "poor disbanded soldier," as Otway describes himself in the epilogue to *Caius Marius,* has become a new variety of rakehell libertine—penniless as a result of the letters of debenture he was given instead of pay, yet fashionably free-thinking and venturesome. In Otway's mind a soldier is a man of honor and breeding whose life is dedicated to serving his king in battle, like the knights of the medieval romances. Expert in the arts of war and love, these grandsons of the old Cavaliers preserve all the finest traditions of the English aristocracy. Otway even chose to permit himself to be addressed as "Captain Otway," following his military service, so strongly did he identify with this chivalric ideal.

Lest anyone remain unaware of the financial difficulties his misadventure with the army had imposed upon him, Otway dedicated this play to his publisher, Richard Bentley, in these unusually plain words:

For, Mr. Bentley, you pay honestly for the Copy; and an Epistle to you is a sort of an Acquittance, and may probably be welcome; when to a Person of higher Rank and Order, it looks like an Obligation for Praises, which he knows he does not deserve, and therefore is very unwilling to part with ready Money for.[19]

More precisely, as Courtine explains in the play, this ill fortune is closely connected to the troubled times. We hear the voice of Otway himself, cursing his scurvy fortune in now-familiar terms:

Of all Strumpets Fortunes the basest; 'twas Fortune made me a Souldier, a Rogue in Red, the grievance of the Nation; Fortune made the peace just when we were upon the brink of a War; then Fortune disbanded us, and lost us two Months pay: Fortune gave us Debentures instead of ready Money, and by very good Fortune I sold mine, and lost heartily by it, in hopes the grinding ill natur'd dog that bought it will never get a shilling for't.

"Loyalty and starving are all one," Beaugard explains, "The old Cavaliers got such a trick of it in the Kings Exile, that their posterity could never thrive since." Otway was working feverishly this season to repair the state of his finances; the previous autumn he had brought forth *Caius Marius,* and *The Poet's Complaint, The Orphan,* and *The Soldier's Fortune* all followed within the next six months.

In this comedy Beaugard's solution to *his* reverses of fortune is to take employment with Sir Jolly Jumble, an elderly pimp. The old man is such an ambitious businessman that "rather than want employment, he will go from one end of Town to t'other to procure my Lords little Dog to be civil to my Ladies languishing Bitch." A "reverend Vice" like Falstaff, Sir Jolly considers himself to be "as good a natur'd publick spirited Person as the Nation holds; one that is never so happy as when he is bringing good people together, and promoting civil understanding betwixt the sexes." Beaugard's joining his ranks of escorts sets familiar machinery of Restoration comedy in motion, exchanging sex for cash, exalting "honest" opportunists while bringing the hypocrites to grief. The play moves all around the city of London of 1680, from the popular "Blew Posts" tavern to the Mall in St. James's Park. The characters include a covey of prostitutes, a professional killer, some aristocratic ladies, a foolish old merchant aspiring to a position in the city's new Whig power structure, and some constables. A rich network of contemporary allusions provides variations on the theme of opportunism, for political corruption meshes with personal intrigue, and public and private exchanges of "favors" for a price collaborate to form one vast maze of social prostitution.

Because Beaugard, the hero, believes sensibly in survival, he opens the play by persuading his friend Courtine to follow his own decision to become a part of Sir Jolly Jumble's escort service: "thou hast other vices enough for any Industrious young fellow to live comfortably upon" without resorting to actual thievery. Being an escort, he reasons, cannot be all that bad: "surely an Old Ladies Pension need not be so despicable in the eyes of a disbanded Officer, as times go." But he carefully explains that it is a point of honor with him never to marry, "for though we may make bold with another mans Wife in a friendly way, yet nothing upon compulsion Dear-heart." Beaugard thereby joins the ranks of the libertine-Machiavels of Wycherley and Etherege, who seek the means to satisfy their natural appetites without sacrificing their natural freedom to society's corrupt demands.

Though his need for money is painfully real, Beaugard considers himself an unemployed gentleman. In one mellow reminiscence at the Blew Posts, he muses, "Ah, Courtine, must we always be idle? must we never see our glorious days again?" The army is his true profession and he longs to see duty again, to the point of looking forward eagerly to the day when Louis XIV stirs up war:

Ay, now we are at home in our natural Hives, And sleep like Drones; but there's a Gentleman on the other side the Water, that may make work for us all one day.

For the moment at least, they are drone bees in the hive of the city, living only to serve the female and doing nothing else.

The female in Beaugard's case is one Lady Dunce, the pretty young wife of Sir Davy Dunce, an old "paralytick, coughing, decrepid Dotrell." When he meets her in person, Beaugard is taken aback to learn that his first client is the very girl he had been courting before he was sent overseas. At first he wants no part of the arrangement for he suspects that she merely wants to make a fool of him, but she succeeds in convincing him that her husband is the fool in this game. Cleverly, she manages to engage Sir Davy in arranging her rendezvous and even delivering her love-tokens, all to Beaugard's great relish. At heart, he is dismayed by her marriage. Even though she protests that "the Perswasion of Friends and the Authority of Parents" forced her into matrimony, he is contemptuous: "And had you no more Grace, than to be rul'd by a Father and Mother?" It is Beaugard's custom to think his way through his predicaments, living by his wits, in order to remain true to the principles he has chosen. "No compulsion" is his watchword, and as long as he retains his independence, he is no man's slave. But Clarinda, Lady Dunce, finds that the stupidity of her husband allows her some measure of freedom of action, as her song explains:

> Yet old men Profit bring as Fools bring ease,
> And both make Youth and Wit much better please.

Sir Davy is, of course, a thoroughly ridiculous character, a lampoon of the bourgeois Whig merchant who sees an opportunity to become powerful—and rich—in the new City Party. He is hopelessly repetitious and forgetful in his speech, the combined result of his advanced years and dim wit. The muddle of prejudices which serves as his political philosophy further reveals his superficiality. He fears Jesuits with a passion, and retails wild stories about their infiltration of the country: "Yes to my knowledge, there were several at Hounslow Heath disguised in dirtie Petticoats, and cry'd Brandy. I knew a Serjeant of foot that was familiar with one of them all night in a Ditch, and fancy'd him a woman, but the Devil is powerful." Sir Davy possesses a fine gold medal and a chain which he proudly says he "took from the Roman Catholik Officer for a Popish Relick." He is tight-fisted with his money, habitually estimating aloud the value of items and pondering how he might strike a profitable trade or sale. When in the course of the play he hires a ferocious assassin, one Bloody-Bones, to murder Beaugard and learns that the usual fee for such a task is £200, he objects so violently that the project is scaled down from murder to a beating— at half the price. He is as cowardly as he is mercenary, furthermore, and so the very presence of Bloody-Bones terrifies him into a condition of twittering servility. The promise of Beaugard's heart served up for breakfast causes him to gasp, but the assassin insists, "Why your Algerine Pirates eat nothing else at sea, they always have them potted up like Venison, your well-grown Dutchmans Heart makes an excellent Dish with Oyl and Pepper."

Otway had Falstaff in mind when creating the character of Sir Jolly Jumble, the most convivial apostle of vice ever to cross the stage. His exuberance seems as boundless as his erotic enthusiasm is universal. He lusts after the young men he employs, calling them, "My Hero! my darling! my Ganimede! how dost thou? Strong! wanton! lusty! rampant!" He addresses Sylvia and Lady Dunce in the same manner as he chatters with his flock of whores, in a barrage of sexual endearments: "Come hither, Hussie, you little Canary-bird, you little Hop o' my Thumb!" It is his particular pleasure to observe, either from under the bed or through the special peephole he has bored through the wall separating his house from the Dunces', the assignations which he has so solicitously arranged.

. . . Ah my little Son of thunder, if thou hadst her in thy arms now between a pair of sheets, and I under the Bed to see fair play. Boy, gemini! what wou'd become of me? What wou'd become of me? There would be doings, oh, Lawd, I under the bed!

Anthony Leigh was acclaimed for his acting in this role, pinching and tickling and kissing, relentlessly chattering this special brand of nonsense in a steady flow of restless energy. Like Falstaff, Sir Jolly is proud of his "vocation" of pimping. From his point of view, marriagebroking is the truly disgraceful profession. "I won't be seen in the business of Matrimony, 'tis a damn'd invention worse than a Monopoly, and a destroyer of civil correspondence." In defending his *Short View* from critical attack by William Congreve, it is not surprising that Jeremy Collier cites *The Soldier's Fortune* as a high example of "Lewdness and Irreligion."[20] One cannot deny that Sir Jolly is a thoroughly lewd character both personally and professionally. It is not surprising that within a few decades his part was removed from the play.

Sir Jolly and Sir Davy in tandem provide the moral poles of *The Soldier's Fortune.* The former represents sexual opportunism, the latter political and financial opportunism. The business of matrimony falls in the second category, so Beaugard sides with Sir Jolly and his "principles" in working out a tolerable business arrangement. He thoroughly enjoys his work for Lady Dunce, naturally enough, and he takes additional satisfaction in making a fool out of Sir Davy. Like Goodvile, Sir Davy stands for truly mean-minded exploitation. He thinks he is willing to hire a murderer to avenge his nonexistent honor, but he is too cheap to pay the two hundred pound fee. When he is deceived into believing that Beaugard *has* been murdered, and he will have to pay for it after all, he goes into an orgy of terrified praying—for himself. Desperate, he considers running away and going into hiding, until Sir Jolly impishly reminds him that such an act would involve forfeiting his estate, which of course is unthinkable. Then when Sir Jolly offers to dispose of Beaugard's "body," Sir Davy swiftly concocts a scheme to have *him* found with the corpse and charged with the crime. The hastily summoned constable parts the bedcurtains as Sir Jolly's house, to reveal Beaugard, very much alive, with Lady Dunce enjoying a "feast of Love." Sir Davy is ridiculously relieved: "I am a Cuckold, . . . any body may make bold with what belongs to me, ha, ha, ha; I am so pleas'd, ha, ha, ha, I think I was never so pleas'd in all my life before, ha, ha, ha.' "

The only discordant note is struck at this point by the betrothal of Sylvia, Sir Davy's ward, to Courtine, Beaugard's friend. It is an evil omen for the future that Sir Davy profits by five thousand pounds upon Sylvia's dowry just because Courtine impetuously—"upon compulsion" of love—vows he will marry without the old fool's consent. This scene represents Otway's intuition, which proves correct, that the Sir Davys of this world will continue to thrive and profit as long as social institutions continue to perpetuate moral hypocrisy.

Those who claim that this play lacks moral substance are concentrating upon the sexual playing-field and ignoring the careful design of the playwright. True immorality, in Otway's view, lies in the cowardly willingness to perjure, swindle, and even murder for the sake of property and preferment. Sir Davy is the epitome of all that the loyal Otway despised, and surely the success of *The Soldier's Fortune* during the Exclusion Crisis years turned upon the highly satisfying—and highly visible—cuckolding of that obnoxious Whig. His Puritanical pretensions of religion and honor combine with a sly treachery born of cowardice and miserliness, to make him a perfect emblem of middle-class depravity.

Restoration audiences could not have missed this point, familiar as they were with the bourgeois buffoon. Only the changing circumstances which eventually brought forth middle-class critics could lead to the sort of tight-lipped observation Professor Ham makes upon this play:

Granted an audience of elegant savagery, the antics of Sir Jolly and Sir Davy must have been exceedingly diverting. . . . Lady Dunce, on her part, throughout displayed not a shred of conscience. The game of sex, the light give and take so entertaining in Etherege . . . had now become a downright serious business. And in contrast to Otway's tragedy, there was not in his comedy a single decent woman—at least for long. The world was in an endless ferment of lust unsatisfied, satisfied, nauseated, the most striking note of which was the entire consistency of its operation.[21]

The Tory playwright, first of all, sees the new Protestant rebels as the true savages. Though he roundly condemns the practice of selling one's freedom for financial security in marriage, he refuses to condemn mere sex as long as there is "no compulsion." Lady Dunce is not quite believable to Beaugard when she claims to be the victim of her parents' arrangement, but the fact that she has been married off to Sir Davy does not necessarily require her fidelity. She is not a "decent" woman in Professor Ham's terms—chaste if unmarried, faithful if married.

Many of Otway's plays, serious and comic, deal quite explicitly with a great range of sexual behavior. Unquestionably this display of what subsequent generations have come to label perverted and sickening sex preoccupies, even engrosses, those who condemn his plays. In addition to the theme of rape in tragedy and the coupling and cuckolding in comedy, Otway deals with homosexuality, voyeurism, male prostitution, fetishism, and sadomasochism, all of which have been declared disgusting and have successfully distracted Puritanical attention away from the other moral implications of the plays. Just as the Nicky-Nacky flagellation scenes in *Venice Preserv'd* were pruned from the text to the detriment of the play's moral balance, *The Soldier's Fortune* lost Sir Jolly Jumble. Since this reverend vice is responsible for arranging most of the action, it is difficult to imagine how the censored version could make any sense. Obviously he was removed because of his own aberrant sexual preferences, but it is these very preferences which make him such an impeccably professional pimp and such a genuinely human erotic reincarnation of Falstaff. To sympathize with Sir Davy, as for example in wishing Lady Dunce to show some conscience over her infidelity, is simply silly. It is also a grievous critical misjudgment which only betrays an identification with those Whig values Otway detested. Though the Whig cause eventually triumphed, gratitude for the rights and privileges it won for the middle class must not overshadow some of the less admirable features of the Whig heritage—meanness with money, enforced piety, and sexual repression.

Chapter Five

After the Playhouses Merged (1682–1683)

Venice Preserv'd

The stage history of *Venice Preserv'd*, recounted in Aline Mackenzie Taylor's *Next to Shakespeare,* reveals this tragedy to have been "most popular when political feeling was most strongly partisan."[1] Apparently the direction of that feeling mattered less than its intensity. One curious example of political paradox reveals that the British soldiers stationed in New York in 1777 under General Howe called for a revival of *Venice Preserv'd* as an expression of their Tory sympathies, while in the same year, in London, the play was banned for its "dangerous republican tendencies."[2] Certainly at the time of its first performance in February 1682, partisan feelings were running high. Otway's loyal prologue celebrates the Tory sense of ascendancy of the moment by alluding to the death of the Popish Plot. And yet the nature of the play itself transcends immediate issues, because the pattern of injustice and sequence of betrayals retains a universal pertinence.

The best way to begin an analysis of *Venice Preserv'd* is to examine this system of betrayal, for it is the foundation of the plot. Belvidera, the daughter of a Venetian senator, has given her heart and hand to Jaffeir against her father's wishes, after Jaffeir had risked his life to save her from drowning. When the play opens, they have been married long enough to have a child, but the old senator's bitterness has not eased: he has, in fact, just succeeded in obtaining a legal commission to seize all of the couple's property. Jaffeir's trusted friend, a soldier named Pierre, explains that this abuse of power is typical of the oppression of the Senate:

> The Laws (corrupted to their ends that make 'em)
> Serve but for Instruments of some new Tyranny,
> That every day starts up to enslave us deeper.

Pierre urges Jaffeir to join a conspiracy to overthrow the Senate. He too has a personal grievance, for he discovered his mistress in the arms of the "rank, old bearded" senator Antonio, and when he chased him away he was summoned to the Senate for public censure—on the grounds of violation of privilege.

Pierre's mistress, the courtesan Aquilina, still loves him though he is disgusted with her, and so she permits him to use her house for a meeting-place for the conspirators. Jaffeir is introduced by Pierre as trustworthy. To prove his good faith, Jaffeir volunteers Belvidera and his dagger as pledges to the conspirators, with the injunction, "And with her this, when I prove unworthy— / You know the rest:—Then strike it to her heart." Belvidera is taken to the apartment of the chief conspirator, Renault, who attempts to rape her. Jaffeir is so outraged to hear of this betrayal of his trust, that he cannot manage entirely to conceal his disgust with Renault when the conspirators next foregather. Renault, for his part, tries to persuade the others that Jaffeir is unreliable and should be killed to assure silence, but Pierre forges a reconciliation of purpose.

Next Belvidera persuades Jaffeir to save Venice from what she sees as horrible "bloudshed, rapines, desolations" by informing the Senate of the plot. He agrees, and when he is arrested delivers the names of the conspirators to the Senate with full details of the insurrection, on the condition that the lives of the plotters be spared. The Senate gives its pledge of mercy, but in bad faith. The conspirators are arrested. The Senate has twice betrayed Jaffeir at this point, the conspirators once. Pierre, brought before him in fetters, repudiates Jaffeir and strikes him. He is contemptuous of the plea-bargaining Jaffeir has attempted and he returns the dagger, calling it a "worthless pledge."

Belvidera brings news that the conspirators will be tortured to death the next day, and Jaffeir broods upon the dagger. Cursing her as a traitress, he tries to stab her as he had promised—"when I prove unworthy"—but finds that he cannot bring himself to do it. He orders her to seek the mercy of her father. She does so, distraught, and further persuades the old man that the conspirators' lives must be saved if hers is to be spared. Meanwhile Pierre's mistress Aquilina also persuades the old Senator Antonio, with torture, to spare Pierre's life.

Jaffeir parts forever from Belvidera, blessing her this time instead of cursing her, and she begins to lose her mind. Pierre and Jaffeir apologize to and forgive each other, resuming their oath of friendship unto death even while the wheel of torture is being readied for Pierre. All the other conspirators are dead. Pierre requests that Jaffeir stab him instead of allowing him to die dishonorably, and Jaffeir does so just as Pierre is bound to the rack. He stabs himself as well. Belvidera arrives, now totally mad, and sees their ghosts rising "together, both bloody": she dies of distraction.

In this remarkable sequence of events, which resembles an artfully constructed row of dominoes whose utter collapse is precipitated by a single fall, it is the contradictions which are most astonishing. This play seems to be so different from *Alcibiades*, where the hero has one dimension of loyalty: although he had betrayed Athens for Sparta before the play began, Alcibiades is not vulnerable to the shifting circumstances surrounding him, as Jaffeir is. Yet *Venice Preserv'd*, like *The Orphan*, is wholly indebted to the heroic tradition.

In heroic tragedy, dramatic action must express the movement of the passions of the soul. As Dryden observed again and again,

To express the passions which are seated in the heart, by outward signs, is one great precept of the painters, and very difficult to perform. In poetry, the same passions and motions of the mind are to be expressed, and in this consists the principal difficulty, as well as the excellency of that art. . . . Mr. Otway possessed this part as thoroughly as any of the Ancients or Moderns.[3]

By the passions, Dryden means those attributes of the soul, or mind, which suffer experience and impel action, as in the Cartesian or Hobbesian psychology. The strange Platonism, yearning for a commingling of souls after death, which characterizes many heroic dramas, is intended to illustrate the highest aspirations of the lofty soul. We have noted that Otway abandons the neo-Platonic convention after his first two plays. Cartesian passion psychology argues that the lofty soul struggles toward an understanding of God and directs the passions toward this end through the operation of right reason. But Otway deliberately refuses to link psychology with religion in this fashion: thus we have the repudiation of the Chaplain in *The Orphan* and Pierre's refusal to accept the consolation of the Priest in *Venice Preserv'd*. "You want to lead my Reason blindfold," Pierre accuses.

Heroic tragedy therefore is the drama of the divided soul in which passions become actions under the supervision of the will. It portrays a world of warring powers and conflicting desires, a world at war with itself. Its characters consistently establish relationships which divide their loyalties: two friends love the same woman, lovers belong to rival families, a king spares the life of a traitor at the request of his son whose own life the traitor had saved, and so on. Reconciliation prepares only for another separation, as the cells of the plot divide and divide again. Always the relationships are clearly defined though hopelessly complicated by circumstance, for heroic characters appraise themselves and analyze the state of their souls with utter candor. In these terms Jaffeir appeals to Belvidera for absolution she is unable to give:

> Take me into thy Armes, and speak the words
>   of peace
> To my divided Soul, that wars within me,
> And raises every Sense to my confusion.

As dilemma follows dilemma, the process of making decisions is always of supreme importance, for the mind is forever contemplating itself, questioning, testing, and suffering, while the will must act. Jaffeir carefully analyzes the passions storming in his heart after Pierre has struck him in the face and returned his "worthless" dagger:

> What shall I doe? resentment, indignation,
> Love, pity, fear, and mem'ry how I've wrong'd
>   him,
> Distract my quiet with the very thought on't
> And tear my heart to pieces in my bosome.

This passage becomes clearer viewed through the lens of passion psychology. Resentment and indignation are both forms of hatred: resentment is hatred directed toward those who have attacked us, while indignation is a more general species of hatred toward evil-doers. A quick resentment is more noble than slow, smoldering resentment, and both Pierre's slap and Jaffeir's hasty anger fall into this category. Fear is one manifestation of desire which always looks toward the future, and it occurs when desire for good recognizes that the possibility of attainment is slim. Pity is a form of sadness commingled with love or goodwill. The three forms of benevolent love, as opposed to concupiscent love, are affection, friendship, and devotion. Degrees of esteem are responsible for this differentiation. Affection is directed toward those we esteem less than ourselves, while friendship is shared with equals. Devotion reflects the highest esteem: it is the form of love in which we esteem ourselves less than the person or principle loved, so that we are willing to sacrifice even life in its behalf. Jaffeir's speech at this point shows his friendship subliming into devotion. He must forsake Belvidera as a result of choosing the greater principle involved in his oath to Pierre.

While the passion psychology may sometimes lead to a hero who is nearly paralyzed by a moral impasse, like Don Carlos, Jaffeir is from the first established as a man of action. Because of this natural inclination, he makes mistakes, suffers indignities, changes his mind, and even criticizes a woman—all in pursuit of honor. Most remarkable of all is his betrayal of the conspiracy upon which he had pledged his dagger and his wife. Some critics, like Addison, believe that a conspirator by definition simply cannot be heroic:

This poet has founded his tragedy of *Venice Preserv'd* on so wrong a plot, that the greatest characters in it are those of rebels and traitors. Had the hero of his play discovered the same good qualities in the defence of his country, that he showed for its ruin and subversion, the audience could not enough pity and admire him. . . .[4]

Addison is using pity in the psychological sense of sadness mingled with goodwill, so that his classification of Jaffeir and Pierre as traitors rather than, say, revolutionary heroes forbids admiration.

Aline Mackenzie Taylor believes that critical dissatisfaction with *Venice Preserv'd* stems from disapproval of the essentially personal nature of the motivation.[5] She points to the personal or domestic emotions which incite Jaffeir to act—anger at his father-in-law's rejection, outrage at the attempted rape of his wife, and anger at himself for capitulating to the demands of a woman. The code of honor which binds Jaffeir and Pierre, symbolized by the dagger, is the key to understanding the temperamental variety of the tragedy.

But Jaffeir is meant to be a great and lofty soul. He responds just as passionately to the general as to the personal predicament, and his place at the center of rapidly shifting civil turmoil inevitably affects him both as a citizen and as a private individual. His father-in-law's vindictiveness is a typical example of the arrogance of the Senate in its corrupt use of legislative power for personal revenge. His decision to join Pierre in the conspiracy to overthrow the Senate is only partially founded upon the personal passion of anger—the general passion of indignation at the oppressions of government operates here as well. Later, when Belvidera describes Renault's attempted assault, Jaffeir is personally outraged, but his decision to report the conspiracy is not based exclusively upon personal vengeance. Belvidera's "general" argument that it is wrong to injure and kill, no matter what the cause, combines with his personal disappointment to lead him to seek what he hopes will be a bloodless resolution. Therefore he carefully demands of the Senate a full pardon for himself and the other rebels in exchange for giving the details of the plot. To be sure, the corrupt Senate has no intention of keeping its promise of amnesty, but by now we are aware of the ways in which Jaffeir's sense of responsibility always drives him to act rather than retreat, and how, at the same time, his own sense of honor requires him to assume that others will behave with decency.

The first thing we learn about Jaffeir is that he saved Belvidera from drowning. The political and domestic situations in the tragedy unfold in rapid sequence, so that each shift in the moral setting has some particular urgency for Jaffeir the rescuer, once he has pledged himself to help save Venice from drowning in corruption. He is not unthinkingly rash or impetuous, but the circumstances of imminent revolution require swift action. It is the great irony of the play that coming to recognize the world's depravity may lead a man of honor to destroy his last hope of redeeming it: as in *The Orphan,* there is always the possibility that it is past redemption.

Jaffeir's weakness is his lack of cynicism and his inability to anticipate the worst that may befall him in any given situation. In this respect he is the antithesis of Polidore, whose weakness is pessimism. The rescuer necessarily accepts the risks he faces in saving a drowning person and assumes automatically that the imperiled victim is worthy of saving. The Golden Rule ultimately requires the faith that others are

like yourself. When they are not, you may find yourself a martyr in a
world without honor and justice. In *Venice Preserv'd* there is no doubt
that the wicked inherit the earth. Jaffeir curses them all as he dies:

> Now, ye curs'd Rulers,
> Thus of the blood y'have shed I make Libation,
> And sprinkl't mingling: May it rest upon you,
> And all your Race: Be henceforth Peace a
>   stranger
> Within your Walls; let Plague and Famine waste
> Your Generations—oh poor Belvidera!

It has been understandably difficult for some critics to accept Jaffeir
as a hero. He is first a rebel, then a traitor: he loves his wife, yet he
curses her and even tries to kill her. How can those paradoxes exist in a
man of honor? Jaffeir is not to be understood as a model Tory, nor,
Addison to the contrary, does this play glorify traitors and rebels. *Venice
Preserv'd* presents us with a new kind of hero caught up in the moral
crises universally inherent in civil war: Jaffeir is torn between old and
new loyalties, repeatedly forced to distinguish between his love for
individuals and his love for humanity. His soul is too sensitive to be
successfully partisan, as it becomes aware of the shadows of evil to be
found on all sides, and yet he does not retreat from responsible action.
He acts according to each situation, and when finally he confronts the
depths of his own moral schizophrenia, kills his friend to save him from
dishonor and kills himself in his own behalf.

Just as Jaffeir resembles Castalio, the wronged brother in *The
Orphan,* Pierre resembles Polidore. Pierre's commitment to the conspiracy is total, and he acts upon his choice with military dedication.
Though he is thoroughly contemptuous of social institutions—the law,
marriage, religion—in the manner of the Restoration libertine, he is
chivalric in his devotion to the sanctity of his word. The oath of loyalty
shared with Jaffeir is a sacred principle with him. His censure by the
Senate for "violating something they call priviledge" intensifies his
sense of deep dishonor:

> A Souldier's Mistress Jaffeir's his Religion,
> When that's prophan'd, all other Tyes are
>   broken,

> That even dissolves all former bonds of service,
> And from that hour I think my self as free
> To be the Foe as e're the Friend of Venice—
> Nay, dear Revenge, when e're thou call'st I am
>   ready.

As for conventional religion, Pierre has no time for it. In the final scene before he is stretched on the rack, he discharges the priest who has been sent to offer him comfort, assuring him that his conscience is clear and does not need the "blindfold" of religion.

Like the twins in *The Orphan,* the heroic friends complement each other as if they represented two sides of a single personality. One is utterly rational and unsentimental, the other is sensitive and passionate. They share a loyalty which transcends the world's vicissitudes, and yet they can only work toward self-destruction. Polidore goads Castalio into killing him, so that he may atone for his crime, and Jaffeir does the same for Pierre.

Otway's fondness for patterns of opposing pairs of characters is also apparent in the two women in the play. Belvidera is the virtuous daughter, wife, and mother: Aquilina is the Greek courtesan. The former is the quintessence of submissiveness, while the latter is shown as independent and even sexually dominant. Belvidera, with her frail and tender nature, seems to invite victimization by her very presence. She describes Renault's assault:

> No sooner was I lain on my sad Bed,
> But that vile Wretch approacht me; loose,
>   unbutton'd,
> Ready for violation: Then my Heart
> Throbb'd with its fears: Oh how I wept and
>   sigh'd,
> And shrunk and trembled; wish'd in vain for him
> That should protect me. Thou alas! wert gone!

Aquilina, on the other hand, is shown accepting a purse of gold from Antonio in exchange for abusing him: "Come Nacky, Nacky, lets have a Game at Rump, Nacky." In this controversial scene, we witness the old Senator pretending to be a bull, asking her to spit in his face, and finally crawling under the table barking like a dog while she kicks him about and finally brings forth a whip and drives the ecstatic Antonio out of the house.

The contrast is maintained when Jaffeir has betrayed the plot, and the lives of the conspirators are in peril. Belvidera rushes to her cruel father to implore him:

> Oh, you would take me in your dear, dear Armes,
> Hover with strong compassion o'r your young one,
> To shelter me with a protecting wing,
> From the black gather'd storm, that's just, just
>   breaking.

She melts her father's heart completely with her helplessness. In the next scene, we find Aquilina bargaining in her way for the life of Pierre. She holds a dagger to Antonio's throat, to his intense delight. "Swear to recall his doom, / Swear at my feet, and tremble at my fury." To which Antonio replies voluptuously, "I do; now if she would but kick a little bit, one kick now Ah h h h."

The scene in which Belvidera persuades Jaffeir to inform on the plot is steeped in the language of pain and torture. In urging him to avenge her honor, she adds an image of horror should the insurrection take place, including the screams of murdered infants whose mothers stand helplessly by, their breasts dripping with blood and milk. Jaffeir is swayed by her appeal and agrees to forewarn the Senate, but significantly he compares himself to a sacrificial lamb accompanying a priestess to the slaughter:

> The wanton skips and plays,
> Trots by the enticing flattering Priestess's
>   side,
> And much transported with his little pride,
> Forgets his dear Companions of the plain,
> Till by her, bound, Hee's on the Altar layn,
> Yet then too hardly bleats, such pleasure's
>   in the pain.

She is the priestess of tribal loyalty, utterly incapable of understanding her husband's commitment to the cause. Jaffeir hates her for using his love to destroy his self-respect and manhood, but she can only sense his loathing without comprehending it. When he reclaims his dagger, along with his self-esteem, and parts from her forever, she loses her mind.

Belvidera was canonized by subsequent generations of theatergoers, while the Nicky-Nacky scenes were excised for being too offensive for the stage. Since the psychological development of the tragedy moves by contrasts and parallels, such editing for the sake of decorum necessarily destroys the balance of the moral pattern. Belvidera must not be the central figure here—Jaffeir must. And yet in terms of social history the exaltation of female passivity requires the repudiation of female aggression. Revulsion over the flagellation scenes shifts the emphasis to a sensual enthusiasm for torturing the helpless female, which can only be seen as secretly sadistic. Renault's attempted rape is therefore judged to be proper or acceptable to the terms of the play, but Antonio's erotic enthusiasm for punishment is improper. One can easily see how a sentimental interpretation alters the sadomasochistic element in the plan in a manner that destroys Otway's careful and delicate design. Such is the power of the sentimental movement that even twentieth century critics like Roswell Gray Ham are heard to observe admiringly, "Otway's women are ever stronger than his men."[6] He explains that he alludes here strictly to the tragic ladies and not the indecent women of the comedies. One wonders whether the rapes which are pivotal in both *The Orphan* and *Venice Preserv'd* are interpreted by such sentimentalists as unrelated to lust—or whether, perhaps, a strong woman is necessarily a raped woman. In any case, the interpretation of Otway's plays, like many of their Restoration counterparts, has been seriously distorted by the social conventions and mores of the eighteenth and nineteenth centuries, not to exclude our own.

The imagery of fire and water, like the choreographical pairing of the characters, further reflects the war between action and passivity. Belvidera and her father had been watching the annual spectacle of the Duke of Venice wedding the Adriatic Sea, when she was "by a Wave washt off into the Deep." Both elements are included in the conspirators' plan to fire the city:

> How lovely the Adriatique Whore,
> Drest in her Flames, will shine! devouring
> Flames!

> Such as shall burn her to the watery bottom
> And hiss in her Foundation.

Pierre accuses the Duke of Venice of cowering timorously in his palace while an invading navy was allowed to attack the city:

> And saw your Wife, th'Adriatick, plough'd
> Like a lewd Whore by bolder Prows than yours.

When Jaffeir determines to take action to reclaim his sullied honor, even though it means leaving Belvidera to fend for herself, he thinks in terms of fire:

> Bend down, ye Heavens, and shutting round this
>   earth,
> Crush the Vile Globe into its first confusion;
> Scorch it, with Elemental flames, to one curst
>   Cinder,
> And all us little creepers in't, call'd men,
> Burn, burn to nothing . . .

Belvidera, ever the passive principle, uses the watery imagery of tears and rain as she approaches her final madness:

> How I could bleed, how burn, how drown the
>   waves
> Huzzing and booming round my sinking head,
> Till I descended to the Peacefull bottome!

Indeed in her delirium, embracing Jaffeir's corpse as she dies, she senses herself drowning:

> My Love! my Dear! my Blessing! help me,
>   help me!
> They have hold on me, and drag me to the bottom.
> Nay—now they pull so hard—farewell—

Jaffeir's struggle to act honorably leads him through the three stages of the passion of love, from affection for those weaker than himself to friendship for Pierre, his equal, and ultimately to devotion, when he finds at last the principle of honor for which he willingly sacrifices his life and grants his friend a noble death. This evolution takes place by means of carefully poised contrasts. He curses Belvidera when she obliges him to betray the conspiracy, but when he regains his awareness, he is benevolent and gentle toward her. His soul is divided by Pierre's insult, yet he becomes grateful and apologetic when he recognizes that he is still capable of one last action which will restore that which is most dear to him, his honor.

Otway excels in the exploration of the "pleasure in the pain" as a strong yet paradoxical motivating force in human behavior. The complexity and excellence of this tragedy, despite the damage its reputation has suffered through the distorted exaltation of Belvidera, causes the reader to join with those who mourned Otway's untimely death. He had achieved in *Venice Preserv'd* a moral vision of tragedy in startlingly modern terms, unsentimental in overall design, existential, and yet affirming the potential nobility of man in a wholly ignoble world.

The Atheist

The Atheist: or, The Second Part of the Soldier's Fortune was Otway's last play before his death. It has received little critical attention, perhaps because it seems to be only partially finished and therefore is a disappointment after *Venice Preserv'd*. But Otway's comedies have always received short shrift, just as his tragedies have been exalted, and many have claimed to find it difficult to believe that the "tender Otway" could take the jaundiced view of humanity required by a "Plain Dealer."

The play is dedicated to the eldest son of the Marquess of Halifax with a plea for his protection: "for indeed it has great need of such Protection: having at its first coming into the World met with many Enemies, and very industrious ones too." The dedication is remarkable for praising the father instead of the son, commending Halifax's brave opposition to Shaftesbury, who died in exile in Holland half a year before the play was performed. According to the dedication, it was Halifax who:

when all manner of Confusion, Ruin and Destruction, was breaking in upon us, like the Guardian Angel of these Kingdoms, stood up; and with the

Tongue of an Angel too, confounded the Subtleties of that Infernal Serpent, who would have debauched us from our Obedience, and turned our Eden into a Wilderness.

The Tories were fond of this image of Shaftesbury as Satan ever since John Dryden had borrowed heavily from Milton to show the Whig leader "Sagacious, Bold, and Turbulent of Wit" inspiring evil ambitions in the breast of young Monmouth:

> A fiery soul, which, working out its way,
> Fretted the pigmy body to decay,
> And o'er-inform'd the tenement of clay. [7]

In celebration of Shaftesbury's death, Charles and James were treated to a performance of Dryden's *Albion and Albanius* before a special backdrop depicting

a man with a long, lean, pale face, with fiend's wings, and snakes twisted round his body, accompanied by several fanatical rebellious heads, who suck poison from him, which runs out of a tap in his side. [8]

Otway's dedication is his contribution to the general Tory rejoicing as much as it is the usual polite requisition of funds.

The prologue rails at the amateur competition in the realm of poetry, which Otway believes to be all the more outrageous since the playhouses joined and thereby narrowed the opportunities for new productions. These "poetasters" are too stupid to appreciate a good play when they see one, he says, and he concludes by threatening to write down to their level:

> Else is our Author hopeless of Success,
> But then his Study shall be next time less:
> He'll find out Ways to your Applause, more
>   easie;
> That is, write worse and worse, till he can
>   please ye.

Although he had the advantage of the familiar talents of Betterton and Smith as Beaugard and Courtine, Mrs. Barry as Porcia, Underhill as Daredevil, and Leigh as Beaugard's old father, the play is imperfect in a number of ways, so that Otway's prologue seems to be a defense.

The lovers of the first part of *The Soldier's Fortune* were never of great consequence to that plot: that Sylvia and Courtine should turn up to be disappointed in their rancid marriage now is of no great consequence to this one except as a device to initiate the action. Courtine is in the last stages of disillusionment with marriage, like the husband in Hogarth's *Marriage à la Mode*. He has come to London hoping to share some of Beaugard's bachelor adventures, and asks for a briefing on "what Sins are stirring in this Noble Metropolis."

Why, 'faith, Ned, considering the plot, the Danger of the Times, and some other Obstructions of Trade and Commerce, Iniquity in the general has not lost much Ground. There's Cheating and Hypocrisie still in the City; Riot and Murder in the Suburbs; Grinning, Lying, Fawning, Flattery, and False-promising at Court, Assignations at Covent-garden Church; Cuckolds, Whores, Pimps, Panders, Bawds, and their Diseases, all over the Town.

Courtine's wife, Sylvia, unbeknownst to him, has tracked him to London out of jealousy and frustration: she is staying with her cousin Porcia, Beaugard's mistress. Porcia learns that Sylvia is starving for affection and devises a little scheme to bring Courtine to his unsuspecting wife. Sylvia confides her unhappiness to Lucrece, a woman who is secretly in love with Beaugard and therefore jealous of Porcia. Her portrait of marriage is also Hogarthian:

He's colder to me, than Adamant to Fire; but let him loose amongst my Kitchen-Furniture, my Maids, never was seen so termagent a Towzer: . . . To be despis'd at that rate, so dishonor'd makes me even curse the Chance that made me Woman: Would I had been any Creature else.—

Lucrece sees the opportunity to do mischief and, as if inspired by Sylvia's suggestion, dresses herself as a man for that end. Her purpose is to prepare Sylvia for seduction, then to lead Beaugard to Sylvia's room and Courtine to Daredevil's. Admiring her masculine appearance, she muses:

Let me see; I have a hundred and a hundred times wish'd my self a Man; and now, in outward appearance, I am a very Fellow; nay, a very pretty Fellow: for, methinks Foppery, Impertinence, Self-conceit, and other Masculine Qualities grow upon me strangely.—

Sylvia is utterly susceptible to Lucrece's bold advances and therefore finds Beaugard in her bed eventually: but Lucrece's plot is foiled because neither Beaugard nor Porcia is dismayed by the misadventure; both fall happily into one another's arms. Lucrece is not given time to voice her chagrin. Otway simply whisks her offstage with a parting jibe at Courtine, and she never returns. She is a potentially interesting character, another example of Otway's exploration of sexual aberrance, but she is left unfinished.

The same is true of Beaugard's old reprobate of a father. A lecherous, alcoholic, gambling dotard whose only motive in effecting a reunion with his son is mercenary, Beaugard's father deserves a comeuppance which never materializes. The first act carefully explores the myriad ways in which he has abused and exploited his son for his own gain, then abandoned him when he no longer had money to lend him for gambling. Beaugard's uncle has just bequeathed him a sum of £2,000 per annum, which explains the old man's return to his son. Presuming upon his "right" to demand filial allegiance, he interrogates Beaugard upon the subject of marriage and religion. Beaugard is cool but civil in his reply:

But, Sir, to make short of the matter, I am of the Religion of my Country, hate Persecution and Penance, love Conformity, which is going to Church once a Month, well enough; resolve to make this transitory Life as pleasant and delightful as I can; and for some sober Reasons best known to my self, resolve never to marry.

The old man is pressing his son to marry while he has the fortune to attract a wealthy wife, in hopes that the merger will provide him with gambling money to the end of his days. Beaugard's plan is simply to let the old man run up debts, "that to avoid the Calamity, he shall be forced to compound with me for his Freedom, and be contented with a comfortable Annuity in the Country." In the fifth act, for no reason logical to the plot, Beaugard's father disguises himself as a "Phanatique Preacher" to extort a confession of sins out of the Atheist, a scene written for the farcical gifts of Leigh and Underhill more than a natural outgrowth of the motivations of the characters.

The atheist of the title, Daredevil, is a weak character who boasts that he fears no afterlife, and yet when he is slightly wounded in a scuffle, falls to praying and confessing his sins—a stock and single joke. Unlike Sir Davy Dunce, whose night of terrified praying is hilarious because so many of his pretensions are collapsing about his ears, Daredevil is a sketchily developed character. He is well established in the first two acts, however, suggesting that Otway rushed his comedy to a premature and superficial conclusion. In the second act, Courtine opines that fear of hell is a restraint on wicked behavior and Daredevil, who claims that his god is the law, replies:

Fear of Hell! No, Sir, 'tis fear of Hanging. Who would not steal, or do murder, every time his Fingers itch't at it, were it not for fear of the Gallows? Do not you, with all your Religion, swear almost as often as you speak? break and prophane the Sabbath? lie with your Neighbours Wives? and covet their Estates, if they be better than your own? Yet those things are forbid by Religion, as well as Stealing and Cutting of Throats are.

His conversion, when he believes he is dying, is not convincing; he confesses to whoring and drinking, he gibbers and whines with fear of dying, but he never proclaims to see the light, as Lord Rochester allegedly did.

Rochester's deathbed conversion and repentance of sins had taken place three summers before *The Atheist,* under the watchful supervision of Bishop Burnet, who soon published an account of the remarkable event. Members of the court who had known him well were not convinced of his sincerity, however, and inclined to the belief that he had simply at last gone mad.[9] Both the severity and nature of his illness, compounded with the quantities of laudanum administered to him at the end, makes this assumption plausible. And yet, because there is no accounting for miracles, no one can be completely sure. News of the conversion was promptly dispatched through "thousands of harangues, Urg'd with grimaces, fortify'd with bangs, On dreadful pulpits."[10] Otway would most likely on these grounds, that the reformation served as Whig propaganda, be suspicious of the report.

There are other weaknesses in the structure of the play as well, including an improbable masque. Porcia, masked, leads Beuagard and Daredevil to an "enchanted" bedchamber where Beaugard is undressed by two exotic black ladies and attended by a dwarf who talks mysteriously about "the Power I serve" and the "Spirits of the Air" which guard this crystal castle. He is fed little dainties by two cupids and then teased by the masked lady into confessing his love for Porcia. This elaborate scene, complete with musical interludes, must have been intended to put the fear of hell into Daredevil as well as to show Beaugard's true feelings for Porcia, but Otway becomes absorbed in the romantic and lyrical possibilities of his masque to the neglect of the comic ones.

The heart of the play, Beaugard's romance with the widow Porcia, who despises marriage as much as he does, is "finished" and well worth study. As a girl, Porcia had been married off by her guardians who were eager by this means to obtain her fortune:

In short, to give you one infallible Argument that I will never marry, I have been married already, that is, sold: for being the Daughter of a very rich Merchant, who dying left me the onely Heiress of an immense Fortune, it was my ill luck to fall into the Hands of Guardians, that, to speak properly, were Raskals; for in a short time they conspired amongst themselves, and for base Bribes, betray'd, sold, and married me to a—Husband, that's all.

When her husband died, he left her money, but arranged to have it administered by his tyrannical brother, Theodoret, who literally made a prisoner of her when she refused to marry him. She has escaped his clutches without a penny, but Theodoret and his sidekick Gratian are scouring London for her. Just as Beaugard's father's interest in his son's marrying is purely motivated by money, Porcia's sad story reveals how a well-to-do woman may be easily victimized by the arrangements of marriage.

As a match for Beaugard she is ideal. Marriage appalls her because she has been victimized and exploited by it, and yet as a "lady in distress," which she calls herself, she appeals directly to Beaugard's soldierly nature. Her two relatives by marriage are threatening that freedom which she insists is "an English Woman's natural Right. Do not our Fathers, Brothers and Kinsmen often, upon pretence of it, bid fair for Rebellion against their Soveraign; And why ought not we, by their Example, to rebel as plausibly against them?" Earlier in the play when she explains her perilous situation to Beaugard, Porcia says:

Murder and Marriage are the two dreadful things I seem to be threatned with: Now guess what pity it is that ever either of those Mischiefs should fall upon me.

Yet when it comes to a forced choice between the two, she turns to Beaugard:

> If now you think it worth your least Regard,
> Protect me; for I dread my Brother's Fury,
> Ev'n worse than Matrimony. Here, Sir, I
>   yield my self
> Up yours forever.

Beaugard brings a party of soldiers to the house where Porcia is imprisoned and literally lays siege to the stronghold. He has a "flying Party" and a squad to lure the enemy within the garden walls. This is war, and Porcia trusts him:

> This shall, in after Story, be call'd,
> Captain Beaugard's beseiging of the Widow.
> Which, as 'tis laid sure, with Success must
>   end,
> Since Justice does his Enterprize attend
> Without, and powerful Love within's his Friend.

He proves to be a most competent strategist, for he succeeds in taking over the house. He announces to Theodoret:

This Lady is in my Charge now, and you in my Power; and by her Authority, this being her own house, I have made thus bold with it, and will take care to dispose hereafter out of the reach of your merciless Tyranny; nay, if this reverend person will do us the friendly office, though I have often renounc'd it, am ready to do it one way this moment. Daredevil, wilt thou lend me thy Chaplain?

The Chaplain in question is none other than Beaugard's father, who has been amusing himself at the atheist's expense, and so of course no marriage ceremony can take place at that moment. Beaugard describes himself as "beginning to settle my Family." This involves a contract which will provide his father with three bottles of sack a day, two pounds of tobacco a month, beef and beer for dinner, a pretty young servant, spending money, "an old Pacing Horse" and an easy chair for the rest of his days. Beaugard assumes responsibility for Porcia: "I have taken this Lady off from your Hands, and intend to make her another sort of Domestick." Theodoret and Gratian are to remain imprisoned until Porcia is formally secured, and "for the other part of the Family, I care not to make Excuses."

This is Otway's resolution of the problem of love, and for the first time in a comedy of his we find his main attention focused upon an honest match. Beaugard is not the kind of gallant who must settle for a marital truce, since he and Porcia are not at war with each other. He marries her for her safety and protection. Conquest is the goal of the true soldier and Beaugard triumphs like the lover in *The Romance of the Rose* when he captures the imprisoned and endangered lady. The lady freely gives her love to him and would even prefer not to marry—it is only because she has been taken prisoner by a society which exploits its institutions to capitalize on her material assets that Beaugard's drastic action is required to set her free.

This chivalric view of love preserves honor where a typical Restoration business deal does not. Professor Ham believes that "Beaugard, the hunter of womankind, was himself trapped into matrimony" and "the whole vicious circle had only recommenced."[11] It is possible to disagree with this view. Beaugard freely assumes marriage, and Porcia's confidence in his love and in the justice of his cause shows that she is willing to marry him in good faith. Throughout the play, the lovers demonstrate great concern and compassion for each other, making it very difficult to say that this is a revoltingly cynical play—instead, it is strangely optimistic.

Theodoret is the unquestioned villain. He and Gratian are heartlessly abusing Porcia on the grounds of a dubious and tenuous family (read financial) tie. It is his sort, which treats people like property, that represents the enemy. Otway expresses throughout this play a thorough contempt for family associations, which he sees as officially sanctioned bondage covered over with sanctimonious propaganda. Just because his dead brother had purchased Porcia as his wife from her unscrupulous guardians and had transferred the management of her portion of his estate into his hands, Theodoret assumes that she is now his property. When she refuses to marry him and escapes instead to the city, he is outraged: he is obsessed with the idea that she is a whore, and freely rails at her. When she asks him civilly, "Why am I abus'd thus?" his reply is hateful:

Theo.	For the same reason other too hot blooded Females are; because, if possible, I would not have a good Breed spoil'd.
Porcia.	What a Load of Dirt is the Thick Skull cramm'd withal, if the Tongue were able to throw it out!
Theo.	Filthy, filthy, fulsom filthy! What, be a Doll-Common, follow the Camp! How lovelily would your fair Ladyship look, mounted upon a Baggage-Cart, presiding over the rest of the Captain's dirty Equipage.

He attempts to take her by force then, but Beaugard's father intervenes. Theodoret's grossness, callousness, and violence can only be stopped by more violence. Therefore Beaugard, the soldier without a war, rises to the challenge, brings Theodoret to his knees, and takes him prisoner.

Thus it is that in this last badly finished play we find the "bawdy" and "cynical" Otway demonstrating that the rare virtues of honor and decency may still be found to exist in a society populated with fools, rascals, and villains, as long as there are people who are willing to show courage and a concern for others which transcends their own self-interest.

We know that Otway's serious plays are often considered to represent the transition between heroic drama and sentimental drama. Critics who study Otway wishing to prove this link are often disappointed with his comedies and puzzled by their (sexual) immorality. But it is not so difficult to resolve this mystery of how the creator of Monimia and Belvidera, the favorites of the sentimental, could also give us so many unchaste and unrepentant women in comedy. Otway was totally out of sympathy with the Puritan Whigs, and with all the other values of the bourgeois and commercial mind. Therefore his comic heroes refuse to play into the hands of the Dunces because they are the loyal heirs of the "old Cavaliers" who "got the trick of starving in the Kings Exile." In reading *The Atheist,* for all its structural weaknesses, we find Otway clearly spelling out the old chivalric ideals of military valor, loyal friendship—even saving a lady in distress from a contemporary dragon.

Sentimental comedy compromises with bourgeois values, but Otway's obviously does not. Since the moral basis of his comedy is the loyal and chivalric ideal blended with the free-thinking libertine's scourge of folly, no compromise is possible. Otway was on the losing side of the Glorious (bourgeois) Revolution. It has been the Whig critic, after all, who has on the one hand exalted Monimia and Belvidera nearly to sainthood and, on the other, prudishly edited Nicky-Nacky and Sir Jolly Jumble. For nearly three hundred years Whig Squeamishness has reigned supreme. It has focused narrowly upon the sex in Restoration comedy and declared it nauseating or boring, when it was meant to be funny. Whig critics are not amused by attacks on their religious hypocrisy, or the sanctity of money and legal contracts, or the inviolable holiness of matrimony and family ties: thus they have argued that these plays, like others of the period, reveal an idle and decadent aristocracy when in fact they portray the social traumas caused by the rising middle class.

Otway's condemnation of Whig vices is constantly under our noses, but perhaps we refuse to acknowledge its presence because Sir Davy Dunce is our revered ancestor. Our notions of matrimony, politics, property, religion, and proper behavior are not amusing to us because we are latter-day Whigs. We therefore foolishly wish that Lady Dunce would show "a shred of conscience" over her adultery, and we call for "decent women" while we tolerate the "indecent" bachelor. We admire capitalism and free enterprise in personal relations as well as in the marketplace so much that we condone the violence and suffering committed in its name. That is why, unless we can disengage ourselves from these plays, we find them intolerable. And Otway's comedies are more intolerable to us than Congreve's or Etherege's simply because he more explicitly and consistently was abusing us, the Squeamish, merciless Dunce family.

Chapter Six
Conclusion

With the exception of *The Atheist* in 1683, Otway's work in the last three years of his life consisted of translations, prologues to plays written by friends, and occasional verses. With the market for new plays sharply curtailed by the joining of the playhouses, many writers who had depended on their third nights for a living turned to translating. Dryden is the Restoration's most notably successful translator. At the time of the Glorious Revolution in 1688, Dryden was financially ruined and turned first unsuccessfully to the theater and then to his great translations of Virgil and Chaucer. Otway's experience with this alternative was a failure.

In 1680 Otway contributed an Ovidian epistle, *Phaedra to Hippolytus*, to an anthology printed by Jacob Tonson entitled *Ovid's Epistles, Translated by Several Hands*. Ovid's "soft Genius" was on his mind in the prologue to *Caius Marius* in 1679, as was the theme of incest. Otway's Phaedra writes to Hippolytus, gently declaring her desire for him and presenting him with reasons illustrating that the love of older women for young men is specially blessed by the gods. His interest in sexuality of unusual sorts suffuses the poem with a kind of stealthy, silken ripeness which is simultaneously delicate in expression and glowing with frustrated passion, as befits the character. Phaedra dwells on Hippolytus' untamed appearance and praises his beauty: "Must cold Diana be ador'd alone? / Must she have all thy Vows, and Venus none?" She lets him know that her husband is away and her bed is cold. Her desire mounts as she writes, so that she rationalizes the matter of incest:

> Mother and Son are notions, very Names
> Of worn out Piety, in fashion Then
> When Old dull Saturn Rul'd the Race of men:
> But braver Jove taught pleasure was no sin,
> And with his Sister did himself begin.

By the end of the letter she explains that her amorous passion has reduced her to a suppliant: "Now on my own, I crawl to clasp thy knees; / What's Decent no true Lover cares or sees." Ending her letter with the wish that he may never "love a scornful fair," she paints a picture of his beloved forest where he quenches his thirst from a stream, and tells him of the millions of tears that flow from her eyes as she writes this letter. It is apparent from the theme, and from the imagery of the hunt, that *The Orphan* was also on Otway's mind.

In 1683 Otway published a poem commending another translation, *To Mr. Creech Upon his Translation of Lucretius*. "Lucretius English'd! 'twas a work might shake / The powr of English Verse to undertake." Not only does the Epicurean philosophy represented by Lucretius align neatly with Otway's eloquent libertinism, Creech's poetical strength is great enough to match the ancient poet's challenge:

> Still with him you maintain an equal pace,
> And bear full stretch upon him all the Race.

The first third of the poem is straightforward, honest praise—not the sort of flowery style reserved for panegyric, but a frank appreciation of the skill manifested by the translation. The rest of the poem is a diatribe against the amateurs and bunglers who are trying to pass themselves off as classical translators:

> When Block-heads will claym wit in Natures
>   spight,
> And every Dunce, that Starves, presumes to
>   write,
> Exert your self, defend the Muses Cause,
> Proclaim their Right, and to maintain their
>   Laws
> Make the dead Antients speak the British Tongue.

He has expressed the same outrage in his prologue to *The Atheist* and will utter the last word on the subject in his prologue to *Constantine the Great*: poor poetry revolts Otway, and its being rewarded at the expense of good verse arouses his most violent indignation.

In the last three years of his life Otway begins to write often about "care." His translation of "The Sixteenth Ode of the Second Book of

Horace" analyzes care, or mental anguish. Peace of mind, or quiet, is the ultimate good which every man seeks. Material wealth cannot buy freedom from care: "wealth and power too weak we find / To quell the tumults of the mind." The poem ends with praise for the hermitage:

> For me a little Cell I chuse,
> Fit for my mind, fit for my muse,
> Which soft content does Best adorn,
> Shunning the Knaves and Fools I scorn.

Otway's most lengthy translation was a 600-page prose work, *The History of the Triumvirates*, from the French work of Sieur de Broe. This work was published after his death, printed by Charles Brome instead of Bentley or Tonson, who had touted the forthcoming book before Otway's death as being "by a judicious hand." Professor Ham finds the prepublication anonymity here to be possibly suggestive that Otway was not proud to attach his name to this kind of hack work.[1] When the book was printed it proclaimed itself to be "written originally in French, and Made English by Tho. Otway, lately deceased."[2] It is generally agreed that this effort, which Montague Summers politely calls "a fluent version of an original which is itself not very attractive,"[3] illustrates the exigencies of poverty above all else.

Otway wrote one epilogue and two prologues in the years 1682–83. A special epilogue honored the Duke of York's attendance at the playhouse on Friday, April 21, 1682. It begins, naturally, with a fulsome compliment to "the injur'd Prince." Next it assails the Whigs and their repeated petitions for Parliaments: Otway labels them all cuckolds and paints a silly picture of their political convocations:

> And when the horned Herd's together got,
> Nothing portends a Commonwealth like *that*.

He mocks their fundraising dinners and the medal they struck to celebrate Shaftesbury's release, then swiftly shifts back into the complimentary mode to offer his good wishes to James's unborn child, "an Infant Prince yet lab'ring in the womb," that he may serve as a pledge "Of Caesar's Love to an obedient Land." The same wishes are expressed in another little occasional poem, the *Epilogue to Her Royal Highness on Her Return from Scotland*, offering allegiance to the unborn child.

Aphra Behn brought forth a comedy in 1682, *The City Heiress, or, Sir Timothy Treatall,* in which she poked fun at the Green Ribbon Men and lampooned Shaftesbury as Treatall. Otway wrote a prologue for this play, which Mrs. Barry recited. A dinner honoring James was the occasion which had inspired the city Whigs to sell tickets to their own counterfeast the next day, and such a furor developed that Charles was obliged to issue a royal proclamation forbidding the Whig assembly. "This Daemon lately drew in many a guest, / To part with zealous Guinny for—no feast." The Tories found the occasion marvelously funny: it was lampooned in *The Whigg-Feast* and *The Loyall Feast* and mentioned in *Absalom and Achitophel.* Otway tried to bring down the house with the following lines mocking the Rye House Plot:

> Who, but the most incorrigible Fops,
> For ever doom'd in dismal Cells, call'd
>   Shops,
> To cheat and damn themselves to get their
>   livings,
> Wou'd lay sweet Money out in Sham-Thanks-
>   givings?
> Sham-Plots you may have paid for o'er and
>   o'er;
> But who e'er paid for a Sham-Treat before?

But it is the prologue to *Constantine the Great,* attributed first to Nathaniel Lee then later to Otway, where Otway has his final word on the frustrations of being a poet. We have discussed the unfortunate circumstances which surrounded the production of this play. Nathaniel Lee's "brain-sickness" was shortly to return him to Bethlehem Hospital, but his friends had rallied to bring *Constantine* to the stage in his behalf. Otway, himself no stranger to poverty and starvation, reasons that when the Creator inspected the earth and pronounced it good, "the Creature Poet was not understood":

> 'Tis plain they ne're were of the first Creation,
> But came by meer Equiv'cal Generation.
> Like Rats in Ships, without Coition bred;
> As hated too as they are, and unfed.

His sympathy for Lee's plight has its source in his own "cares": he alludes to "the Starving Sign of Capricorn," his own birth sign. Advising parents to spare no pains in discouraging their sons from aspiring to be poets, Otway offers some advice, beginning "This last Experiment, O Parents, make!" Professor Ham is too squeamish to record it in his biography, saying:

But we need not continue with the savage last suggestion set down by Otway, inasmuch as it was dictated by an age more outspoken than our own.[4]

The offending passage follows:

> Then lead him to some Stall that does expose
> The Authors he loves most, there rub his Nose;
> Till like a Spaniel lash'd, to know Command,
> He by the due Correction understand,
> To keep his Brains clean, and not foul the Land.
> Till he against his Nature learn to strive,
> And get the Knack of Dullness how to thrive.

His outrage can only be properly expressed in scatological terms.

In his *Epistle to R.D. from T.O.*, Otway is in a quieter state of mind, but his cares are very much with him. This poem expresses his great affection for his friend Richard Duke of Cambridge and tells of a dream-visit wherein the two men fish, relax, read, and share pleasant suppers together with their mistresses. Still keenly interested in the workings of the mind, Otway includes this allegorical but revealing passage:

> And there methinks, Fancy sits Queen of all;
> While the poor under faculties resort,
> And to her fickle majesty make court.
> The Understanding first comes plainly clad,
> But usefully; no ent'rance to be had.
> Next comes the Will, that Bully of the mind,
> Follies wait on him in a troop behind;
> He meets reception from the Antick Queen,
> Who thinks her Majesty's most honour'd when
> Attended by those fine drest Gentlemen.

His tone of contempt for Fancy indicates that he is using the term in the strict psychological sense of delusion, as in Wycherley's poem to Lee in Bedlam, "Your Fancy now, does all your Wants supply." Delusion grants an audience to Will and his troop of Follies, but drives away Understanding. Otway's dream, he realizes, is Fancy:

> Reason, the honest Counseller, this knows,
> And into Court with res'lute vertue goes;
> Lets Fancy see her loose irregular sway,
> Then how the flattering Follies sneak away!
> This Image when it came too fiercely shook
> My Brain which its soft quiet streight forsook.

When he awakens to find "no grove, no freedom, and . . . no friend," his thoughts fall prey to "their old Tyrant Care." The diverting of Care provokes the poem, which concludes with a prayer for peace of mind, along the lines of the sixteenth ode of Horace.

> But grant me quiet, liberty and peace,
> By day what's needful, and at night soft ease.

At this late date it is impossible to ascertain exactly what Otway meant when he described himself as lacking "freedom" and "liberty." It is possible that he was confined in a sponging-house at this time, a sort of preliminary prison maintained by a bailiff for debtors. It is also possible that Otway alludes to mental fetters rather than physical ones. In any case, there can be no question of his despondency or the struggles he is having with the old tyrant Care when he concludes the epistle with the charge to the gods, "But make Life what I ask, or tak't away."

On February 6, 1685, while Otway was engrossed in translating the *History of the Triumvirates,* Charles died. In the two months before his own death, the poet wrote two elegies commemorating the king. *A Pastoral on the Death of His late Majesty* is a short, rather clumsy poem which was printed in a miscellany of poems in 1688. It takes the pathetic fallacy of mourning nature through thirty lines of pastoral platitudes, including nymphs suffering convulsions and larks who have forgotten to announce the dawn. Even the elegiac refrain is awkward:

> The Royal Pan, the Shepherd of the sheep,
> He who to leave his Flock did dying weep,
> Is gone! is gone, ne're to return from death's
>   eternal sleep.

"The Royal Pan," suggesting faintly the pleasure-loving traits of the dead king, is the only phrase in the poem which reveals Otway's graceful wit: it cannot save the poem.

But *Windsor Castle, in a Monument to K. Charles II* is a finished and moving elegy in praise of the late king's "Celestial Mind." After an account of the troubles which plagued the reign and a description of the mildness and mercy which Charles displayed toward his ruthless opposition, "when this Land in Bloud he might have laid," Otway draws the central analogy of the poem comparing the ancient castle at Windsor to the godlike mind of the king. The poet was invited to Windsor on the king's birthday and was "curious to see what Fame so far had spread," for Charles had undertaken the building of "Britain's Olympus" at the venerable site.

The tour begins with the old and hallowed St. George's Church, a "Reverend Dome" which contains the smaller St. George's Chapel honoring the memory of the dead Knights of the Garter. A guide explains their banners on the walls:

> Those Banners rais'd on high
> Betoken noble Vows of Chivalry,
> Which here their Hero's with Religion make
> When they the Ensigns of this Order take.

Otway's reverence for the chivalric ideal, which kept his own loyalty intact and caused him to seek out at one point a military career, is inspired anew by the scene. The thought of St. George as a dragon-killer and a model of honorable behavior, combined with this shrine of knighthood, leads him to question his own cynicism:

> For I had been told all Vertue was but Show
> That oft bold Villany had best Success,
> As if its Use were more not Merit less.
> But here I saw how it rewarded shin'd.

His preoccupation with the strumpet Fortune and his anguish at
finding his poetry going unrewarded walk beside him like personal
Furies as he wanders into a small neglected cell which is filled with a
jumble of dusty trophies. This place, his note explains, is "an old Isle in
the Church where the Banner of a dead Knight is carried when another
succeeds him." He broods about the men whose hatchments lie there in
disarray:

> But what his Recompence? A short Applause,
> Which he ne'er hears, his Memory may grace,
> Till, soon forgot, another takes his Place.

The playwright instinctively thinks of eulogies in terms of "unheard
applause."

The meditation continues in a brilliant summation of his tragic view
of life, poised as it is in a setting of uncertainty and shifting values, the
pawn of chance, fate, and fortune. It is as if Otway sensed that he was
writing here the epilogue to all of his plays and the valediction to his
own despairing life as well as to Charles's troubled reign.

He rouses himself from his daydream and moves on to inspect the
Keep, the original fortress-prison which seems to keep watch over all
the buildings at Windsor. Next Otway is invited into the castle to
admire the new paintings by Sieur Verrio which had been commissioned by the king:

> Through all the lofty Roofs describ'd we finde
> The Toils and Triumphs of his Godlike mind.

The monumental hall "where St. George's Feast is kept" is splendid
with the reminders of the country's great rulers. Edward the Third is
painted as he greets the returning Black Prince in triumph after his
French conquest. In the Chapel at the end of this hall Verrio has painted
the Ascension which Otway delicately, so as not to blaspheme, compares to the Restoration. Charles's heavenly gift of wisdom has enabled
him to do homage to the creator with these great paintings, Otway
reasons: it was heaven as well which tried the king's soul with banish-
ment before restoring him in triumph to his throne.

The concluding portion of the poem follows the Restoration fashion
of "Advice to a Painter":

> Thus far the Painter's Hand did guide the Muse,
> Now let her lead, nor will he sure refuse.
> Two kindred Arts they are, so near ally'd,
> They oft have by each other been supply'd.

Otway directs Verrio's hand to paint the distempered Parliament entangled in "bold Tumults and Disorders," with Charles preparing to disperse them by means of his scepter. The second scene must show the sorrowing court at the king's deathbed, with James embracing his brother fondly. The third painting must depict the happy reign of James the shepherd, on the one hand keeping his "Contracted Foes" at bay, while on the other benevolently supervising a scene of pastoral serenity. Thus the poem ends appropriately with good wishes for the new king as well as a warning for his enemies:

> But Heav'n such Injur'd merit did regard,
> (As Heav'n in time true Vertue will reward)
> So to a Throne by Providence he rose,
> And all, who e'er were his, were Providence's Foes.

Perhaps Otway was fortunate to have been spared the experience of seeing his hopeful prophecy for the new reign fail to materialize. For all the free-thinking skepticism of his comedies and all the existential mutability of his serious plays, Otway's loyalty to the house of Stuart seems to have been a principle of faith: *credo quia absurdum est*. It makes no difference that experience should have demonstrated to him by this time that such virtue could not find reward either in the judicious epistle dedicatory or on the battlefield. Otway defends this one principle to the death.

Returning to the passage in which he ponders the fate of the supplanted knight, and of himself, we see him in effect anticipating death.

> And happy that Man's Chance who falls in time,
> E'er yet his Vertue be become his Crime;
> E'er his abus'd Desert be call'd his Pride,
> Or Fools and Villains on his Ruine ride.
> But truly blest is he whose Soul can bear
> The Wrongs of Fate, nor think them worth his Care:

Whose Mind no Disappointment here can shake,
Who a true Estimate of Life does make,
Knows 'tis uncertain, frail, and will have end,
So to that Prospect still his Thoughts does bend;
Who, though his Right a stronger Power invade,
Though Fate oppress, and no man give him Aid,
Cheer'd with th'Assurance that he there shall
     find
Rest from all Toils, and no Remorse of mind;
Can Fortune's Smiles despise, her Frowns out-
     brave;
For who's a Prince or Beggar in the Grave?

Two months later, Otway was dead. "1685. Thomas Otway, a man, buried 16 April," reads the parish register. "But what his Recompence? A short Applause, which he ne'er hears. . . ." In his case, the unheard applause continued for two centuries as he was hailed as "next to Shakespeare" England's greatest playwright. Then the bright sun of his posthumous reputation was eclipsed again. Only a few curious writers have wandered through his effects, preserved now in the rare books rooms of libraries, to find what he had found in St. George's Chapel:

Lo, a Cell,
Where melancholy Ruine seem'd to dwell:
The Door unhing'd, without or Bolt or Ward,
Seem'd as what lodg'd within found small regard.
Like some old Den, scarce visited by Day,
Where dark Oblivion lurk't and watch't for Prey.
Here, in a Heap of confus'd Waste, I found
Neglected Hatchments tumbled on the ground;
The Spoils of Time, and Triumph of that Fate
Which equally on all Mankind does wait.

Notes and References

Preface

    1. Introduction to *The Works of Thomas Otway,* ed. J. C. Ghosh (Oxford, 1932), 1:36.
    2. Introduction to *The Works of Thomas Otway,* ed. Montague Summers, 1:ciii.
    3. Aline Mackenzie Taylor, *Next to Shakespeare* (Durham, N.C., 1950), p. 144.

Chapter One

    1. Montague Summers, *The Complete Works of Thomas Otway* (New York, 1967), 1:xv.
    2. John Downes, *Roscius Anglicanus* (London, 1708), p. 34.
    3. Summers, 1:xxiii.
    4. Thomas Otway, Preface to *Don Carlos,* in *The Works of Thomas Otway,* ed. Ghosh, 1:173.
    5. Roswell Gray Ham, *Otway and Lee* (New York, 1931), p. 54.
    6. Summers, 1:xxxiv.
    7. Ibid., 1:xxv.
    8. *Poems on Several Occasions:* by the Right Honorable, the E——— of R———, Antwerpen (really London), n.d. (ascertained 1680), p. 104.
    9. Ham, p. 92.
    10. A *A Character of the True Blue Protestant Poet: or, the Pretended Author of the Character of a Popish Successor,* folio, 1682, printed for A. Bouks.
    11. Summers, 1:lxxi.
    12. John Verney to Sir Richard Verney, Royal Commission on Historical Manuscripts, 1879, p. 473.
    13. Charles Gildon, *The Laws of Poetry* (London, 1721), pp. 37–38.
    14. Ham, p. 206.
    15. Ravenscroft, Epistle to the Reader, *The Careless Lovers* (1673).
    16. Otway, Dedication to *The Soldier's Fortune,* ed. Ghosh, 2:91.
    17. George Lord, ed., *Poems on Affairs of State* (New Haven: Yale University Press, 1963), 2(1703):132.
    18. Harl. MSS. 7317, pp. 227ff.
    19. *Satyr on the Modern Translators,* in *Dialogues of the Dead,* ed. Alfred Rayney Waller (Cambridge: Cambridge University Press, 1907), p. 47.

20. Ham, pp. 206–209.

21. Harl. MSS. 6913.

22. *A Memorial of Nell Gwynne, the actress, and Thomas Otway, the dramatist,* printed in 1868 by William Henry Hart.

23. Summers, 1:xxv.

24. Ham, p. 176.

25. Cf. n. 18.

26. Ghosh, 1:28.

27. Thomas Shadwell, *The Tory Poets* (London: Printed by R. Johnson, 1682), p. 6.

28. Ham, p. 212.

29. Robert Gould, "The Playhouse, Writ in 1685," *Poems* (London, 1689), p. 175.

30. Summers, 1:lxiv.

31. Ibid., p. xcix.

32. Ham, p. 215.

33. *The Bee,* No. 8, *Works of Goldsmith,* ed. Peter Cunningham (London: John Murray, 1854), 3:128.

34. Thomas Otway, *Heroick Friendship, a Tragedy* (London: A. Mears, 1719), p. 44.

35. Ibid., p. 46.

36. Ham, p. 242n.

37. Anthony à Wood, *Athenae Oxonienses* (London, 1691), 4:170.

38. Charles Gildon, *The Lives and Characters of the English Dramatic Poets* (London, 1699), p. 107.

39. Ham, p. 206.

40. Shadwell, p. 6.

41. Ghosh, 1:37.

42. Otway, Letter 1, ed. Ghosh, 2:475.

43. "The Apotheosis of Milton: a Vision," quoted in Ghosh, 1:34.

44. Wood, p. 170.

45. William Oldys, MS. notes to Langbaine, quoted in Ham, p. 839.

46. Joseph Singer, ed., *Spence's Anecdotes* (London, 1820), p. 44.

47. Joseph Warton, *Essay on the Writings and Genius of Pope* (London: J. Dodsley, 1782), 2:109.

48. Theophilus Cibber, *Lives of the Poets of Great Britain and Scotland* (London, 1753), 2:333ff.

49. Samuel Johnson, *Lives of the Poets,* ed. G. B. Hill (Oxford, 1905), 1:247.

50. John Dryden, *Essays,* ed. W. P. Ker (Oxford, 1926), 2:145.

51. Ibid.

52. William Hazlitt, *Collected Works,* ed. A. E. Waller and Arnold Glover (London, 1903), 5:355.

53. Summers, 1:xx.

54. Ibid., p. lxiv.
55. Ibid.
56. Quoted by Summers, 1:lxxxix. *Fashionable Lectures* (London, 1785), pp. 18–19.
57. Summers, 1:cii.
58. Bonamy Dobree, *Restoration Tragedy* (Oxford, 1929), p. 139.
59. Ibid., p. 145.
60. Ham, p. 183.

Chapter Two

1. David Ogg, *England in the Reign of Charles II* (Oxford, 1934), 2:476.
2. Ibid., pp. 474–75.
3. Ibid., p. 477.
4. Max Beloff, *Public Order and Popular Disturbances 1660–1714* (London, 1939), p. 39.
5. George Macauley Trevelyan, *England Under the Stuarts* (New York, 1946), p. 319.
6. Ogg, 2:597.
7. Trevelyan, p. 338.
8. Ghosh, 2:528n.
9. Ogg, 2:595n.
10. Ibid., 2:611.
11. J. L. Jones, *The First Whigs* (London, 1961), p. 67.
12. Ibid., p. 68.
13. Ibid., p. 106.
14. Ibid., pp. 94–96.
15. Ogg, 2:515.
16. Sir Richard Bulstrode, *Memoirs,* in *Poems on Affairs of State,* 2:xxix.
17. Ibid., 2:196.
18. John Lingard, *History of England* (Philadelphia, 1827), pp. 454–55.
19. See Iris Morley, *A Thousand Lives* (London, 1954), pp. 104–105.
20. Trevelyan, pp. 332–34.
21. Ibid., p. 337.
22. *General Biography; or, Lives of the Most Eminent Persons of all Ages, Countries, Conditions, and Professions Arranged According to Alphabetical Order* (London, 1818), 16:547.
23. Trevelyan, p. 347.
24. Ibid., p. 329.
25. Ibid., p. 346.
26. Edmond Malone, *Life of Dryden* (London: Printed for T. Cadell, jun. and W. Davies, 1800), p. 135.
27. Taylor, p. 57.
28. Ibid., pp. 46–48.

29. Ibid., p. 58.
30. Trevelyan, p. 331.
31. Ibid., pp. 349–50.
32. Dobree, p. 43.
33. Trevelyan, p. 358.
34. Ibid., pp. 350–51.
35. *Spectator*, No. 29, April 14, 1711.

Chapter Three

1. John E. Cunningham, *Restoration Drama* (London, 1966), p. 26.
2. Ibid., p. 27.
3. Ham, p. 44.
4. Clifford Leech, "Restoration Tragedy: A Reconsideration," *Durham University Journal* 11 (1950):106–15.
5. *General Biography*, 16:547.
6. Preface to *Don Carlos*, Ghosh, 1:173.
7. Ibid., p. 175.
8. Ibid., p. 174.
9. Eric Rothstein, *Restoration Tragedy: Form and the Process of Change* (Madison, 1967), p. 86.
10. Ghosh, 1:39.
11. Ibid., p. 174.
12. *Poems on Several Occasions*, p. 104.
13. John Downes, *Roscius Anglicanus* (London, 1708), p. 34.
14. Summers, 1:liv.
15. Prologue to *Scaramouch*, Ghosh, 1:43.
16. Ibid.
17. John Wilcox, *The Relation of Molière to Restoration Comedy* (New York, 1938), p. 80.
18. Ibid., pp. 144–45.
19. Colley Cibber, *An Apology for his Life* (London, 1938), p. 130.
20. Ibid.

Chapter Four

1. Cibber, pp. 86–87.
2. Summers, 1:lxvii.
3. Sister Rose Anthony, *The Jeremy Collier Stage Controversy* (New York, 1966), p. 42.
4. Jeremy Collier, *A Short View of the Immorality and Profaneness of the English Stage* (London, 1698), pp. 100–101.
5. Joseph Wood Krutch, *Comedy and Conscience After the Restoration* (New York, 1924).

6. L. C. Knights, *Restoration Comedy: The Reality and the Myth,* in *Restoration Drama,* ed., John Loftis (New York, 1966), pp. 18–19.

7. Dale Underwood, *Etherege and the Seventeenth Century Comedy of Manners* (New Haven, 1957), p. 93.

8. Ham, p. 106.

9. Epistle Dedicatory, Ghosh, 1:333.

10. Montague Summers, *The Playhouse of Pepys* (New York, 1964), p. 295.

11. Summers, 1:lxxiv.

12. Charles Gildon, *Art of Poetry* (London, 1718), 1:290.

13. Charles Gildon, *Essay on the Art, Rise and Progress of the Stage,* in Rowe's *Shakespeare* (London, 1714), 9:xxxl.

14. Taylor, p. 269.

15. Ghosh, 2:480, Letter 5.

16. Ham, p. 144.

17. Ghosh, 2:481.

18. John E. Cunningham, *Restoration Drama* (London, 1966), p. 27.

19. Ghosh, 2:92.

20. Anthony, p. 139.

21. Ham, p. 105.

Chapter Five

1. Taylor, p. 146.

2. Ibid., p. 202.

3. Dryden, *Essays,* 2:145.

4. *Spectator* No. 39, April 14, 1711.

5. Taylor, p. 39.

6. Ham, p. 193.

7. John Dryden, *The Poetical Works of Dryden,* ed. George Noyes (Cambridge, Mass.: Houghton Mifflin, 1950), p. 111.

8. Trevelyan, p. 351n.

9. Graham Greene, *Lord Rochester's Monkey* (New York, 1974), p. 221.

10. Ibid.

11. Ham, p. 105.

Chapter Six

1. Ham, p. 212.

2. Ghosh, 1:80.

3. Summers, 1:c.

4. Ham, p. 209.

Selected Bibliography

PRIMARY SOURCES

1. Editions of Complete Works

Ghosh, J. C., ed. *The Works of Thomas Otway: Plays, Poems, and Love-Letters.* Oxford: The Clarendon Press, 1968. 2 vols. This edition, originally published in 1932, is generally recognized as textually authoritative.
Summers, Montague, ed. *The Complete Works of Thomas Otway.* New York: AMS Press, 1967. 3 vols. Originally published in 1926, this edition includes the Reverend Summers's inimitably gossipy introduction, over a hundred pages long. Ghosh assails Summers's textual irresponsibilities at some length, and Summers retaliated in 1935, in *The Playhouse of Pepys,* by accusing Ghosh of "completest and most blank ignorance" of the Restoration theater. In addition, he notes that "Mr. Ghosh writes queer English."

2. Editions of Selected Works

Noel, Roden, ed. *Thomas Otway.* London: Vizetelly and Company, 1888. The Mermaid edition of Otway's plays.
Special mention must be made of the Regents Restoration Drama Series separate editions of *Venice Preserv'd,* edited by Malcolm Kelsall. Lincoln: University of Nebraska Press, 1969, and *The Orphan,* edited by Aline Mackenzie Taylor. Lincoln: University of Nebraska Press, 1976.

SECONDARY SOURCES

1. Biographies

Ham, Roswell Gray. *Otway and Lee: Biography from a Baroque Age.* New Haven: Yale University Press, 1931. A useful, careful, and insightful juxtaposition of the two young playwrights' lives. In his preface, Ham carefully notes his utter lack of indebtedness to the Reverend Summers as well as charging the latter of plagiarism, "sometimes verbatim and always with a close similarity of phrase and arrangement." Professor Ham deserves much credit for his efforts in verifying (and discrediting) details of Otway's life.

2. Traditional (though questionable) sources of biographical information.

Cibber, Theophilus. *Lives of the Poets of Great Britain and Scotland.* London: R. Griffiths, 1753. Source of the tale that Otway died choking on bread he had begged for.

General Biography; or, Lives of the Most Eminent Persons of all Ages, Countries, Conditions, and Professions Arranged According to Alphabetical Order. London: G. Smeeton, 1818. This charming encyclopedia, which I discovered in the Huntington Library, sums up the smug compassion of the nineteenth-century view of Otway, wishing that he might have lived in an age with more moral and literary advantages.

Gildon, Charles. *The Lives and Characters of the English Dramatic Poets.* London: T. Leigh, 1699. Alleges that Otway was so fond of drink that he wrote his last poem in its honor.

Johnson, Samuel. *Lives of the English Poets.* Edited by G. B. Hill. 3 vols. Oxford: Clarendon Press, 1905. After asserting that "little is known" of Otway, Dr. Johnson firmly establishes his low opinion of the poet's morals as expressed in his work and his personal life.

Langbaine, Gerard. *An Account of the English Dramatic Poets.* Oxford: Printed by L. L. for G. West and H. Clements, 1691. Praises Otway's plays for being passionately moving and appealing therefore to the ladies.

Spence's Anecdotes. Edited by Samuel Weller Singer. London: W. H. Carpenter, 1820. Source of the legend that Otway caught a fever while pursuing a friend's murderer.

Wood, Anthony (self-styled Anthony à Wood). *Athenae Oxonienses.* London: Printed for Tho. Bennet, 1691. Simple, unornamented account of Otway's life.

3. Critical Studies

Cunningham, John E. *Restoration Drama.* London: Evans Bros., 1966. An examination of the special appeal of Restoration drama in terms of its conventions. Discussion of Otway is rather general.

Dobree, Bonamy. *Restoration Tragedy.* Oxford: Clarendon Press, 1929. Although Dobree interprets Otway as a man ruined by love for an unworthy woman (Mrs. Barry), his analysis is nonetheless memorable for its insights into Otway's theme of abasement and humiliation.

Dryden, John. *Essays.* Edited by W. P. Ker. Oxford: Clarendon Press, 1926. Dryden's singling out Otway's gift for "moving the passions" not only prepares for the sentimental approval of his plays but also reveals the psychological preoccupations of Restoration tragedy.

Gildon, Charles. *Essay on the Art, Rise and Progress of the Stage,* in Rowe's *Shakespeare.* London: Printed for J. Tonson, 1714.

———. *The Art of Poetry.* London: Printed for Chas. Rivington, 1718.

————. *The Laws of Poetry.* London: W. Hinchcliffe, 1721. Gildon's almost unbounded admiration for Otway's tragedies led him to compare Otway favorably to Shakespeare.

Hazlitt, William. *Collected Works.* Edited by A. E. Waller and Arnold Glover. London: J. M. Dent & Co., 1903. Notably impassioned but contradictory criticism of Otway.

Knights, L. C. *Restoration Comedy: The Reality and the Myth.* In *Restoration Drama.* Edited by John Loftis. New York: Oxford University Press, 1966. Affects boredom at Restoration comedy, finding it not " 'immoral' but trivial, gross, and dull."

Krutch, Joseph Wood. *Comedy and Conscience After the Restoration.* New York: Columbia University Press, 1924. Krutch takes the fashionable view for the twenties that Restoration comedy is merely obscene, designed primarily to titillate a jaded aristocracy.

Leech, Clifford. "Restoration Tragedy: A Reconsideration." *Durham University Journal* 11 (1950): 106–15. Leech postulates the escapist appeal of the heroic tragedies.

Rothstein, Eric. *Restoration Tragedy: Form and the Process of Change.* Madison: University of Wisconsin Press, 1967. Valuable study of serious drama of the period.

Taylor, Aline Mackenzie. *Next to Shakespeare.* Durham, N.C.: Duke University Press, 1950. A dazzling work of scholarship, tracing the stage history of Otway's *The Orphan* and *Venice Preserv'd* through the many permutations of their many revivals.

Underwood, Dale. *Etherege and the Seventeenth Century Comedy of Manners.* New Haven: Yale University Press, 1957. Offers depth and breadth of interpretation to the Restoration libertine-Machiavel character.

Wilcox, John. *The Relation of Molière to Restoration Comedy.* New York: Columbia University Press, 1938. Methodically analyzes the degree of Molière's influence on Restoration comedy.

4. Background in the Restoration Theater

Anthony, Sister Rose. *The Jeremy Collier Stage Controversy.* New York: B. Blom, 1966. Reviews the repercussions of the notorious "short view."

Cibber, Colley. *An Apology for his Life.* London: J. M. Dent and Sons, 1938. Recollections of a life in the theater, notable for anecdotes about actors and performances.

Cibber, Colley. *An Apology for his Life.* London: 1938. Recollections of a life in the theater, notable for anecdotes about actors and performances.

Collier, Jeremy. *A Short View of the Immorality and Profaneness of the English Stage.* London: S. Keble, 1699. The Puritan backlash in full feather: Otway is assailed for his lack of respect for the clergy as well as for the immodesty of his ladies.

Downes, John. *Roscius Anglicanus*. London: Printed by H. Playford, 1708. The memoirs of the prompter at the Duke's Theater during the Restoration.

Greene, Graham. *Lord Rochester's Monkey*. New York: Viking Press, 1974. Biography of Lord Rochester, full of magnificent color reproductions of portraits of Restoration celebrities.

Mission, Henri. *Memoirs and Observations in his Travel over England*. London: Printed for D. Browne, 1719. A French observer records his impressions and opinions of the English: notable for its vivid description of the theater.

Summers, Montague. *The Playhouse of Pepys*. New York: Humanities Press, 1964. First printed in 1935. Summers gossips about the world of the Restoration theater as if he had lived in its midst. He also finds the occasion to snipe at Roswell Gray Ham's biography of Otway, calling it "trivially journalistic."

5. Studies of the Period

Beloff, Max. *Public Order and Popular Disturbances 1660–1714*. London: Oxford University Press, 1939. Noteworthy study of the civil dissension of the time.

Jones, J. R. *The First Whigs*. London: Oxford University Press, 1961. A close analysis of the Exclusion Crisis and its political vagaries.

Lingard, John. *History of England*. Philadelphia: Eugene Cumminsky, 1827. Old-fashioned all-purpose history.

Morley, Iris. *A Thousand Lives*. London: A. Deutsch, 1954. An account of the Popish Plot and its fomentors, particularly interesting for its presentation of Whig propaganda.

Ogg, David. *England in the Reign of Charles II*. 2 vols. Oxford: The Clarendon Press, 1934. The definitive history of this period.

Pollock, John. *The Popish Plot*. London: Duckworth and Co., 1903. Not as useful as Ogg or Morley, but important for controversies it provoked.

Trevelyan, George Macauley. *England Under the Stuarts*. New York: Putnam, 1946. First revised in 1925. Trevelyan, like Ogg, is a most readable historian. His sympathies are decidedly on the side of the Whigs' parliamentary aspirations.

Index

Addison, Joseph, 56, 124, 126

Barry, Elizabeth, 5, 7, 15–19, 28–29, 77, 80, 85–86, 90, 103–104, 109, 132
Behn, Aphra, 2, 55, 144
Bentley, Richard, 11, 113, 43
Betterton, Thomas, 15, 18, 20, 72, 103, 132
Borough reform, 33
Brome, Charles, 143
Buckhurst, *see* Sackville
Buckingham, George Villiers, Duke of, 43, 58, 67
Burnet, Gilbert, 45, 135

Charles II, 19, 21, 39, 44–45, 52, 57, 67, 132, 146–49
Cibber, Colley, 75, 86
Cibber, Theophilus, 24
Coleman, Edward, 37, 52
Collier, Jeremy, 88, 108, 117
Commedia dell'arte, 102
Congreve, William, 117, 140
Crowne, John, 5, 72–73, 77
Cunningham, John, 58, 66, 112

Dennis, John, 23
Descartes, Rene, 122
Dobree, Bonamy, 29–30, 53
Downes, John, 2, 4, 27, 67, 72

Dryden, John, 13, 24–26, 58, 62, 67, 93, 102, 132, 141, 144
Duke, Richard, 14–15, 145
Duke's Company, 72, 85
Durfey, Thomas, 93

Essex, Earl of (Arthur Capel), 55
Etherege, Sir George, 70, 79, 89, 114, 140
Exclusion crisis, 34, 39–41, 45–46, 48, 52, 57, 60, 91, 101–102, 118

Fell, Dr. John, 2
Falkland, Lucius Cary, 2nd Viscount, 11
Ferguson, 55
Fielding, Henry, 95

Ghosh, J.C., 22, 30
Gildon, Charles, 10, 103–104
Godfrey, Sir Edmund Barry, 3, 7, 38–39
Gould, Robert, 18
Gwyn, Nell, 5, 11, 14–15, 50

Habeas corpus act, 42, 45
Halifax, Charles Montague, Earl of, 131
Ham, Roswell Gray, 13, 15, 21, 23, 29–30, 58, 90, 118, 129, 138, 143, 145

Hazlitt, William, 26–27, 61
Heroic drama, 58–59, 67, 122–23
Hogarth, William, 89, 133
Horace, 102–103, 143, 146
Howard, Lord, 55

James, Duke of York, 19, 38, 40–41, 44–46, 50, 52, 67, 132, 143–44
Johnson, Samuel, 24, 104
Jordan, Thomas, 6

Knights, L.C., 88
Krutch, Joseph Wood, 88

Lee, Mary, 66, 72
Lee, Nathaniel, 10, 13, 58, 144, 146
Leech, Clifford, 58
Leigh, Anthony, 5, 72, 75–77, 116, 132, 134
Lestrange, Roger, 42
Libertinism, 69–70, 79, 109, 113–14
Licensing Act of 1662, 40, 42, 59
Louis XIV, 41, 47, 50

Marlborough, John Churchill, Duke of, 9
Marvell, Andrew, 43
Massinger, Philip, 50
Meal Tub Plot, 52
Milton, John, 132
Moliere, 5, 72, 75, 77, 85, 89, 102
Monmouth, James Scott, Duke of, 34, 38, 44, 96

Neo-Platonism, 59, 65–68, 71, 90, 122
Nokes, Robert, 72, 93

Oates, Titus, 31, 36–37, 39, 52
Ogg, David, 33–34, 37
Oldys, William, 23
Otway, Thomas, at Oxford, 2–3; military career, 7–8, 113; Cambridge honorary degree, 14; love letters to Elizabeth Barry, 15–19; theme of fortune, 87, 99–100; death, 19

WRITINGS:
Alcibiades, 3, 4, 7, 12, 16, 32, 62–63, 67–68, 72, 91, 105, 122
Atheist, The, 15–16, 20, 131–41
Caius Marius, 2, 8–10, 13, 16, 32, 36, 55, 60, 91–103, 113–14, 141
Cheats of Scapin, The, 5, 72, 75–78
Don Carlos, 4–5, 32, 67–72, 91, 102–103, 124
Epilogue to Her Royal Highness, 143
Epistle to R.D., 145
Friendship in Fashion, 7, 10–11, 16, 75, 77, 79–90
Heroick Friendship (spurious), 20–21, 72
History of the Triumvirates (trans.), 143, 146
Orphan, The, 8–9, 13, 17, 26, 32, 60, 72, 103–112, 114, 122–23, 125–27, 129, 142
Sixteenth Ode, The, (trans.), 142–43, 146
To Mr. Creech, 142
Pastoral on the Death of His Late Majesty, 21, 146–47
Phaedra to Hippolytus, 141
Poet's Complaint of His Muse, The, 1–3, 5–7, 31–32, 36, 38–39,

44, 48, 52, 78, 99, 103, 107,
    114
Prologue to Constantine the Great,
    13, 142, 144
Prologue to The City Heiress, 55,
    144
Soldier's Fortune, The, 8–9, 16, 32,
    47, 75, 113–19, 133
Titus and Berenice, 5, 72–75, 77
Venice Preserv'd, 8, 11, 15–16, 19,
    24, 29–32, 39, 48–58, 61, 72,
    75, 88, 102, 119–31
Windsor Castle, 19, 147–50

Oxford Parliament, 49

Parliament, 34, 42, 47, 49
Passions, 24–25, 74, 77, 122–24
Plutarch, 33, 91, 98–100
Pope, Alexander, 104
Popish Plot, 36–37, 44, 47, 48,
    103, 120
Presbyterians, 41
Propaganda, 42–45

Querouaille, Louise de, 11, 15, 50,
    52

Racine, Jean Baptiste, 5, 72–73,
    77, 102
Ravenscroft, Edward, 5, 11, 72, 75,
    77
Rochester, John Wilmot, Earl of, 4,
    6, 11, 50, 67–68, 78, 86, 135
Rothstein, Eric, 67
Russell, William, Lord, 55–56
Rye House Plot, 52, 55, 144

Sackville, Charles, Earl of Middle-

sex, 4, 11, 87
Saint-Real, l'Abbe, 4, 15
Settle, Elkanah, 4, 6, 8, 9
Shadwell, Thomas, 9, 15, 68
Shaftesbury, 1st Earl of (Anthony
    Ashley Cooper), 32–33, 40,
    51–52, 55, 131, 144
Shakespeare, William, 59–60, 69,
    92–93, 102, 106–107, 110, 112,
    116
Sidney, Algernon, 55–56
Sodom, 6
Sophocles, 105–106, 112
Summers, Montague, 27–28, 30,
    87, 93, 143

Taylor, Aline Mackenzie, 30, 51,
    104, 120
Tonson, Jacob, 15, 143
Tories, 31, 35, 43, 45, 47, 96, 118,
    120, 132, 144
Townshend, 33
Trevelyan, G.M., 46, 56

Underhill, Cave, 93, 132, 134
Underwood, Dale, 89

Verrio, 148

Whigs, 31–33, 35, 39–43, 45–47,
    52, 56, 87–88, 97, 107, 115,
    118–19, 139–40, 144
Whitehall, 46
Wilcox, John, 75
Williams, Joseph, 103
Windsor Castle, 147
Wood, Anthony à, 21, 23
Wycherley, William, 70, 79, 83,
    85, 114, 146

DATE DUE
